HEALTH AND HUMAN DEVELOPMENT

DANTES/DSST* Test Study Guide

971010620143

Published by Breely Crush Publishing, LLC
10808 River Front Parkway
South Jordan, UT 84095
www.breelycrushpublishing.com

ISBN-10: 1-61433-668-7
ISBN-13: 978-1-61433-668-6

Printed and bound in the United States of America.

Table of Contents

Mental Health and Behavior

Usually mental health and behavior are overlooked on the way to the gym in pursuit of a fit body. But mental health is one of the most important aspects of your well-being to consider in determining your quality of life. Mental health is used to describe the thinking part of health. This is just one part of psychosocial health. Psychosocial health includes:

- Spiritual Health – your thoughts about what gives life purpose – the meaning of life, religion
- Emotional Health – your feelings and reactions
- Mental Health – your thoughts, beliefs, attitudes and values
- Social Health – your interactions with others in social situations

Factors that influence psychosocial health include your family situation, the world around you, lifespan and maturity.

Our personality is what makes us unique from other people. It's a dynamic blend of our experiences, heredity, environment and other influences. Our personality determines how we react to problems, stress or other issues.

What is the difference between self-efficacy and self-esteem? Self-efficacy is a term coined by Albert Bandura. It is used to describe a person's belief that they can perform a task successfully, like parenting, attending school or participating in athletics. Self-esteem refers to how much someone values and respects his or herself.

Psychological Approaches

Biological: This theory used for evaluation is based on biology. People who follow this school of thought believe that behavior and personality are linked to their genetics.

Behavioral: To evaluate a person using this approach, one must study and observe behavior. Behaviorists see the individual as a blank slate upon which the impressions of experiences both negative and positive can be recorded.

Cognitive: Cognitive theorists examine how the mind is involved in knowing, learning, remembering and thinking. They study how the mind relates to behavior.

Humanistic: Humanists believe that all people are inherently good and are motivated to achieve their full potential.

Psychoanalytical: This theory revolves around the individual's unconscious motivation.

Structuralism: Created by Wilhelm Wundt. The name comes from his investigation of the elements or "structures" of the mind. He emphasized the importance of the classification of the mind's structures and focused on conscious thought.

Functionalism: William James created this theory. He was interested in the "how" part of behavior. He thought our minds are a continuous flow of information about our experiences. He thought that psychology's role is to study the mind and behavior in adapting to the environment.

Nature vs. Nurture: These two opposing positions are commonly discussed. The Nature concept means that a child will be born with whatever disposition, tastes, and personality that they were "meant" to have, and this concept acknowledges that there are bad seeds. The Nurture concepts means that all children are good; it is the way they are brought up that effects their personality and later, their actions. This is an enduring debate between psychologists.

Counseling Psychology

Freud established a practice for studying and treating patients with psychological difficulties in the 1880s. Although many of his methods and theories have remained highly controversial over the years, no other individual has had such a profound impact on the field of psychology. His psychoanalytic theory became the starting point or basis for many theories which have since developed.

After Freud, many different individuals began developing theories, some of the most important of which include Carl Rogers (who developed the person-centered theory) and Carl Jung. Ironically, both of these individuals studied under Freud, but were disowned by him when they chose to branch off with their own philosophies.

Although these theories were developed and used over the next half-century, what really allowed the counseling psychology profession to take off were the events of World War II. During the war, the military needed an effective method for placing soldiers.

Intelligence and other types of standardized tests began to evolve (initially for the use of vocational counselors) which were used for this purpose. This created a branching of vocational counseling to counseling psychology.

In addition, the events after WWII had an impact on counseling psychology. Many of the soldiers returning from the war suffered two difficulties. Firstly, they needed vocational guidance and training to reintegrate into normal life. Secondly, many suffered from severe psychological distress following the war.

The federal government decided to jointly solve these problems by instituting a division of counseling psychology to work with individuals. The division provided both training and employment for counseling psychologists. It is for these that the field of counseling psychology is considered to have evolved from vocational counseling. The focus of counseling psychology became to help individuals in their daily life struggles, and to teach them both how to be productive members of society, and how to overcome their psychological struggles.

Clinical Psychology

Dorothea Dix, who devoted her life to improving the treatment of mentally ill individuals, made large strides in the development of clinical psychology. Dix originally worked in the field of education. In the mid-1800s, she volunteered to teach Sunday school classes for women in a local prison. It was here that she witnessed the appalling treatment of mentally ill individuals.

At the time, there was little understanding of the causes of mental illness, and even less was understood about its treatment. For example, it was commonly believed that it was entirely untreatable and that mentally ill individuals did not feel pain or cold. As a result, the mentally ill (or, at the very least, those not from wealthy families) were kept in cold, dark cells with little food and in close proximity to all other types of criminals. Often they were whipped or subjected to other forms of disciplinary measures to illicit their compliance. Dix spent the rest of her life working to improve the treatment of mentally ill individuals.

She did this by demonstrating that placing them in caring environments (where they could be watched over and taken care of) would often reduce or eliminate symptoms. Although there was still no scientific understanding of the effects of various mental illnesses, and there would still be a long road ahead before the mentally ill were given truly humane treatment, this was a large step towards increasing interest and improving treatments and attitudes towards it. Due to her work more than 30 hospitals for mentally ill patients were built.

Another important step in the history of treating mental illness was the work of Wilhelm Wundt in the late 1870s. Wundt established the first laboratory for studying the mind, which made it a much more reputable and concrete field. For this he is known as the father of experimental psychology. Wundt's main contribution to the field of psychology was the theory of structuralism.

Schizophrenia

Schizophrenia is a severe mental disease, which affects just over 1% of the world's population. Most patients are diagnosed in their teen years, and almost all are diagnosed before 45. Males have a tendency to develop schizophrenia earlier than females. Schizophrenia is characterized by thinking in illogical and confused patterns, and withdrawing from reality. Some common symptoms of schizophrenia include severe hallucinations, living in fantasy worlds (hearing voices, talking to themselves, etc.), lack of emotion, and disordered thinking. Not every person with schizophrenia experiences each of those symptoms, but they are likely to experience some of them. It's not clear what the exact cause of schizophrenia is. Genetics may play a role, because a person whose sibling has schizophrenia is more likely to develop it themselves. Others believe it is a problem with the brain because studies have shown people with schizophrenia to have less gray matter tissue, and more neurotransmitters.

Suicide

Suicide occurs when a person ends their life. It is the 11th leading cause of death among Americans. But suicide deaths are only part of the problem. More people survive suicide attempts than actually die. They are often seriously injured and need medical care. Most people feel uncomfortable talking about suicide. Often, victims are blamed. Their friends, families, and communities are left devastated.

Why is suicide a public health problem?

- More than 31,000 people kill themselves each year.
- More than 425,000 people with self-inflicted injuries are treated in emergency rooms each year.

Suicide, by definition, is fatal. Those who attempt suicide and survive may have serious injuries like broken bones, brain damage, or organ failure. Also, people who survive often have depression and other mental health problems. Suicide also affects the health of the community. Family and friends of people who commit suicide may feel shock, anger, guilt, and depression. The medical costs and lost wages associated with suicide also take their toll on the community.

Who is at risk for suicide?

Suicide affects everyone, but some groups are at higher risk than others. Men are four times more likely than women to die from suicide. However, three times more women than men report attempting suicide. In addition, suicide rates are high among young people and those over age 65. Several factors can put a person at risk for attempting or committing suicide. But, having these risk factors does not always mean that suicide will occur.

Risk factors for suicide include:

- Previous suicide attempt(s)
- History of depression or other mental illness
- Alcohol or drug abuse
- Family history of suicide or violence
- Physical illness
- Feeling alone

Holistic Health
The holistic approach to medicine is the idea that various factors in a person's life can have an effect on their health. This can include physical health, stress level, family relationships, or work conditions. Holistic doctors are much more likely to try alternative measures such as herbal remedies or acupuncture. The idea does not cure both the disease and the "cause".

Maslow's Hierarchy of Needs

Maslow's Hierarchy of Needs consists of the following stages, from the top down:

- Self-actualization
- Esteem needs
- Belonging and love
- Safety
- Physical needs

These stages begin at physical needs. First you need to have food, water, and shelter before you can worry about other things. Once those needs are met, you may start to think of other things such as safety. You might buy a gun or move to a more prosperous and safe area. Once you are fed, clothed and safe, you will want to meet needs of belonging and love through relationships. If you feel loved, you may begin to think about your self-esteem and how you feel as a person, what you are contributing. The final stage, self-actualization, you may never meet. Most people do not.

Erikson's Developental Stages

Erik Erikson was a psychoanalyst who created stages of emotional growth in regards to human babies. Each stage has different needs and lessons to be learned. If the child or infant does not learn that lesson, he may have a harder time in life down the road. For example, if a baby is crying constantly and is not taken care of, or if it is ignored, it can come to feel mistrust toward others. Another example is the young adult stage. The young adult must deal with either being intimate with someone or deal with feeling isolated. According to Erikson, the most important thing is the development of trust.

Infant *Trust vs. Mistrust*
Infants gain trust and confidence from their caregivers. If those caregivers are warm and responsive, then they will know that the world is good.

Toddler *Autonomy vs. Shame and Doubt*
Children want to choose and decide things for themselves. Autonomy is when the parents give the child that necessary free reign over their choices.

Preschooler *Initiative vs. Guilt*
By playing make-believe, the child discovers who they are and who they can become. They can try their hand at being a princess or a mother or father to their dolls.

School-Age Child *Industry vs. Inferiority*
Children learn to work and get along with each other. Inferiority develops from negative social situations.

Adolescent *Identity vs. Role Confusion*
The adolescent tries many roles to answer the question "Who am I?" and "Where do I fit in society?"

Young Adult *Intimacy vs. Isolation*
Young adults work to create emotional ties and relationships to others. Because of earlier trust issues, some young adults cannot form these attachments and it leaves them isolated.

Middle-Age Adult *Generativity vs. Stagnation*
Generativity deals with leaving something for the next generation. Those that do not do this feel an absence of accomplishment.

Old Age *Ego Integrity vs. Despair*
In this stage, people think about the person that they have become. Integrity comes from achieving what one wanted in life. For those who are unhappy with their past, despair results in fear of death.

Jean Piaget

Jean Piaget (1896-1980) was a biologist who originally studied mollusks (publishing twenty scientific papers on them by the time he was 21), but moved into the study of the development of children's understanding, through observing them and talking and listening to them while they worked on exercises he set. His view of how children's minds work and develop has been enormously influential, particularly in educational theory. His particular insight was the role of maturation (simply growing up) in children's increasing capacity to understand their world; children cannot undertake certain tasks until they are psychologically mature enough to do so. His research spawned a great deal more study, much of which has undermined the detail of his own, but like many other investigators, his importance comes from his overall vision.

Piaget proposed that children's thinking does not develop entirely smoothly, instead, there are certain points at which it "takes off" and moves into completely new areas and capabilities. He saw these transitions as taking place at about 18 months, 7 years and 11 or 12 years. This has been taken to mean that, before these ages, children are not capable (no matter how bright) of understanding things in certain ways, and has been used as the basis for scheduling the school curriculum (Atherton, 2002).1 Piaget is a cognitive theorist. Piaget believed that the individual actively constructs knowledge about the world.

Piaget's Relevant Definitions[2]

Assimilation:

The process by which a person takes material into their mind from the environment, which may mean changing the evidence of their senses to make it fit.

Accommodation:

The difference made to one's mind or concepts by the process of assimilation.
Note that assimilation and accommodation go together. You can't have one without the other.

Classification:

The ability to group objects together on the basis of common features.

Class Inclusion:

The understanding of more advanced than simple classification, that some classes or sets of objects are also sub-sets of a larger class. (e.g. there is a class of objects called dogs. There is also a class called animals. But all dogs are also animals, so the class of animals includes that of dogs).

Conservation:

The realization that objects or sets of objects stay the same even when they are changed about or made to look different. For example, children can understand that the same amount of liquid is in two different shaped jars.

Developmental Norm:

A statistical measure of typical scores for categories of information.

Egocentrism:

The belief that you are the center of the universe and everything revolves around you: the corresponding inability to see the world as someone else does and adapt to it. Not moral "selfishness", just an early stage of psychological development. The move away from egocentrism is called decentration.

Elaboration:

Relating new information to something familiar. An example would be learning how to cook a pasta dish. You may have cooked something similar in the past. In your mind you may think, "This is like that time I made Ramen except now I do…"

Operation:

The process of working something out in your head. Young children (in the sensorimotor and pre-operational stages) have to act and try things out in the real world to work things out (like count on fingers). Older children and adults can do more in their heads.

Recognition:

The ability to identify correctly something encountered before.

Recall:

Being able to reproduce knowledge from memory.

Schema (or scheme):

The representation in the mind of a set of perceptions, ideas, and/or actions, which go together.

Stage:

A period in a child's development in which he or she is capable of understanding some things but not others.

Piaget's Stages of Development

This table was created by James Atherton and defines the different developmental stages according to Jean Piaget.

Developmental Stage and Approximate Age	Characteristic Behavior
Sensory Motor Period (0-24 months)	
Reflexive Stage (0-2 months)	Simple reflex activity such as grasping and sucking.
Primary Circular Reactions (2-4 months)	Reflexive behaviors occur in stereotyped repetition such as opening and closing fingers repetitively.
Secondary Circular Reactions (4-8 months)	Repetition of actions to reproduce interesting consequences such as kicking one's feet to move a mobile suspended over the crib.
Coordination of Secondary Reactions (8-12 months)	Responses become coordinated into more complex sequences. Actions take on an "intentional" character such as the infant reaches behind a screen to obtain a hidden object.

<table>
<tr><td>Tertiary Circular Reactions (12-18 months)</td><td>Discovery of new ways to produce the same consequence or obtain the same goal such as the infant pulling a pillow toward him in an attempt to get a toy resting on it.</td></tr>
<tr><td>Invention of New Means Through Mental Combination (18-24 months)</td><td>Evidence of an internal representational system. Symbolizing the problem-solving sequence before actually responding. Deferred imitation.</td></tr>
<tr><td colspan="2" align="center">The Preoperational Period
(2-7 years)</td></tr>
<tr><td>Preoperational Phase (2-4 years)</td><td>Increased use of verbal representation but speech is egocentric. The beginnings of symbolic rather than simple motor play. Transductive reasoning. Can think about something without the object being present by use of language.</td></tr>
<tr><td>Intuitive Phase (4-7 years)</td><td>Speech becomes more social, less egocentric. The child has an intuitive grasp of logical concepts in some areas. However, there is still a tendency to focus attention on one aspect of an object while ignoring others. Concepts formed are crude and irreversible. Easy to believe in magical increase, decrease, disappearance. Reality not firm. Perceptions dominate judgment. In the moral-ethical realm, the child is not able to show principles underlying best behavior. Rules of a game cannot develop in the mind; only uses simple do's and do not's imposed by authority.</td></tr>
<tr><td colspan="2" align="center">Period of Concrete Operations (7-11 years)</td></tr>
<tr><td colspan="2">Evidence for organized, logical thought. There is the ability to perform multiple classification tasks, order objects in a logical sequence, and comprehend the principle of conservation. Thinking becomes less transductive and less egocentric. The child is capable of concrete problem solving. Some reversibility now possible (quantities moved can be restored such as in arithmetic: 3+4 = 7 and 7-4 = 3, etc.) Classifying logic-finding bases to sort unlike objects into logical groups where previously it was on superficial perceived attributes such as color. Categorical labels such as "number" or "animal" now available.</td></tr>
</table>

Period of Formal Operations (11-15 years)
Thought becomes more abstract, incorporating the principles of formal logic. The ability to generate abstract propositions, multiple hypotheses and their possible outcomes is evident. Thinking becomes less tied to concrete reality. Formal logical systems can be acquired. Can handle proportions, algebraic manipulation, and other purely abstract processes. If $a + b = x$ then $x = a - b$. If ma/ca = IQ = 1.00 then Ma = CA. Prepositional logic present, in as-if and if-then steps. Can use aids such as axioms to transcend human limits on comprehension. Can think hypothetically and test hypothesis. Based on the information in these stages, you can see it is important to have age appropriate materials in school.

Piaget and Freud both agreed that environmental influences could affect the time spent in stages but not the order.

Freud's Psychosexual Stages

Stage	Age	Description
Oral	Birth-1 Year	The new ego directs the baby's sucking activities toward breast or bottle. If oral needs are not met appropriately, the individual may develop such habits as thumb sucking, fingernail biting, pencil chewing, overeating and smoking.
Anal	1-3 Years	Young toddlers and preschoolers enjoy holding and releasing urine and feces. Toilet training becomes a major issue between parent and child. If parents insist that children be trained before they are ready or make too few demands, conflicts about anal control may appear in the form of extreme orderliness and cleanliness or messiness and disorder.
Phallic	3-6 Years	Id impulses transfer to the genitals, and the child finds pleasure in genital stimulation. Freud's Oedipus Conflict for boys and Electra Conflict for girls take place. Young children feel a sexual desire for the other-sex parent. To avoid punishment, they give up this desire and instead adopt the same-sex parent's characteristics and values. As a result, the superego is formed and children feel guilty each time they violate its standards. The relationships between id, ego and superego established at this time determine the individual's basic personality orientation.

Latency	6-11 years	Sexual instincts die down, and the superego develops further. The child acquires new social values from adults outside the family and from play with same-sex peers.
Genital	Adolescence	Puberty causes the sexual impulses of the phallic stage to reappear. If development has been successful during earlier stages, it leads to marriage, mature sexuality, and the birth and rearing of children.

Defense Mechanisms

Defense mechanisms are things that help us relieve stress. We can choose to accept, deny or change our perceptions and feelings to be in harmony with our values. Here is a list of the most common defense mechanisms and what they mean:

Denial:

Complete rejection of the feeling or situation.

Suppression:

Hiding the feelings and not acknowledging them.

Reaction Formation:

Turning a feeling into the exact opposite feeling. For example, saying you hate someone you are interested in.

Projection:

Projection is transferring your thoughts and feelings onto others. For example, someone who is being unfaithful themselves constantly accuses their partner of cheating.

Displacement:

Feelings are redirected to someone else. Someone who has a bad day at work and can't complain goes home and yells at their kids instead.

Rationalization:

You deny your feelings and come up with ways to justify your behavior.

Regression:
Reverting to old behavior to avoid feelings.

Sublimation:
A type of displacement, a redirection of the feeling into a socially productive activity.

Stress and Your Body

The endocrine system is made up of the hypothalamus and other endocrine glands. Endocrine glands create and release chemicals into the bloodstream. The pituitary gland releases hormones that regulate the hormone secretions of other glands. The pituitary gland is located at the base of the skull and is about the size of a pea. Adrenal glands affect our moods, energy level and stress. Adrenal glands also secrete epinephrine-(adrenaline) and norepinephrine.

The nervous system has an area called the Autonomic Nervous System (ANS). The ANS works as an involuntary system; usually, we don't know it is there. Other involuntary systems include respiratory and cardiac functions. Here's the test: if you have to think about doing it, it's not involuntary. ANS is most important in the "fight or flight" response. When we experience great amounts of stress like in an emergency, our body gives us extra energy (adrenaline) to fight, perhaps against an attacker, or to take flight, to run from the attacker. In non-stress times, this system allows us to rest and digest. This system is broken up into three different areas. These are:

- Sympathetic Nervous System: arousing part of the system
- Parasympathetic Nervous System: calming part of the system
- Enteric Nervous System

General Adaptation Syndrome

General Adaptation Syndrome is what happens to our bodies when we experience stress. The general adaptation syndrome has three phases:

- Alarm: what happens when you are exposed to a stressor (late bill, attacker, etc.)
- Resistance: reaction to the stressor and then the process of the body returning to homeostasis (normal function).
- Exhaustion: when the extra energy created by the body is depleted.

Stress is our response to any change. A stressor is anything that causes us to have to adjust to a new situation or change. Adjustment is the term for what we use to cope. For example, someone who handles stress poorly could drink alcohol excessively to compensate or to escape. Strain is what happens to our bodies when we get stressed. Eustress is stress that we can use positively for our personal growth. Some examples of eustress are: getting married, starting a new school or job. Distress is stress that can have a negative effect on us. Some examples of distress are: injury, problems with others, financial problems, or the death of a loved one.

We can also be stressed by our environment. Examples of environmental stress are: background stressors like air pollution or noise pollution, like when a co-worker is playing their radio. You may be unaware of environmental stressors, but they are still there.

Managing stress can seem overwhelming, but there are many things we can do to control it or harness it to good use. When you realize thoughts that are irrational, like worrying about things that are not likely going to happen, you can identify those thoughts and rationally discount them.

Exercise and relaxation are critical positive ways to deal with stress. Eating right will also help you deal with stress – either through the placebo effect of comfort food or by having a healthy diet, which will allow your body to be in top shape.

Managing time is also an effective way to deal with stress. Prioritize your tasks, clean off your desk, do those little things you've been putting off. These cause stress in the back of your mind, creating stress you aren't even aware of having. Some alternative techniques to relieve stress include hypnosis, massage, meditation and biofeedback. The lesser known of these areas, biofeedback is simply a process of self-monitoring through a machine the heart rate, blood pressure, etc., and learning to mentally control them.

Sexuality

The following terminology will be helpful for you to know for the test.

Sexual Identity: recognition of ourselves as sexual beings; a mix of gender identity, gender roles and orientation.
Gonads: the reproductive organs in a male (testes) or females (ovaries)
Puberty: the period of sexual maturation
Pituitary Gland: the gland that controls the release of hormones from the gonads
Gender: your sense of being a man or a woman as defined by your society

Gender Roles: expression of your male or femaleness on daily basis
Gender-Role Stereotypes: generalizations about each gender. For example, men are aggressive and more logical. Women are more nurturing and emotional.
Socialization: process by which a society identifies its expectations
Sexual Orientation: a person's attraction to other people
STDs: Sexually Transmitted Diseases which include AIDS and Herpes.
Heterosexual: attraction to the opposite sex
Homosexual: attraction to the same sex Bisexual: attraction to both sexes
Homophobia: irrational hatred and or fear of homosexuals
Celibacy: not being involved in a sexual relationship
Autoerotic Behavior: sexual self-stimulation, masturbation
Erogenous Zones: areas of the body which, when touched, lead to sexual arousal.

Four stages of the sexual response:

1. Excitement phase
2. Plateau phase
3. Orgasm phase
4. Resolution phase

Human papilloma virus or HPV is considered to be the most common sexually transmitted infections worldwide. This virus is believed to cause most cases of cervical cancer, the second most common cancer for women. Gardasil is an FDA approved vaccine for HPV in women. It is only effective before contracting the virus, and hasn't yet been approved as a vaccine for men.

Vasocongestion is when there is increased blood flow to an area of the body causing an increase in blood pressure and swelling of tissue. Vasocongestion is essential to human sexuality because it is what causes the penis to become erect. However, it also has other applications. For example, blushing is one type of vasocongestion.

Relationships

Emotional availability is the ability to give and receive from other people or a significant other without the fear of getting hurt. This refers to a "connection" between two parties.

There are many different types of families. The one that most people think of when the term is mentioned is the nuclear family – which is composed of two parents and children. There are also what we call extended families, which include grandparents, cousins, etc. Blended families are two families (one or two previously married parents) now combining two households into one.

Parenting styles include the following:

- Authoritarian: "Because I say so" – more prevalent in lower-class families.
- Permissive: Making few demands, hardly ever punishing.
- Authoritative: Respects individuality, but tries to instill social values.

Gerontology

Gerontology is the study of the aging process. Every moment we change, we age and grow a little older and hopefully, a little smarter. As our bodies change, so do our lifestyle and our priorities. People who are working that experience discrimination because of their age, regardless if they are considered too old or too young, are victims of what is called ageism.

Gerontologists have determined three categories of old age:

- Young-old: 65-74
- Middle-old: 75-84
- Old-old: 85+

The elderly are a huge growing segment of the population. This creates many concerns regarding Medicare and Social Security. Will these programs be around for new generations or will they become bankrupt? Another factor that has occurred with the growth of this age group is the need for new businesses focused on the needs and wants of the aged. In-home health care has growth substantially as have other service areas.

Another area of concern is the practice of the elderly purchasing OTC medications without informing their primary physician. While their most common purchases are analgesics, followed by nutritional supplements and laxatives, these can cause interactions with their medications that they are currently taking. Embarrassment and personal discomfort are the main reasons these items are not discussed. Sleeping pills are also common among the elderly. It cannot be stated enough that the patient should discuss any and all medications with their physician and/or pharmacist to ensure they do not experience any drug interactions.

Medicare

Medicare is health insurance for people age 65 or older, under age 65 with certain disabilities, and any age with End-Stage Renal Disease (permanent kidney failure requiring dialysis or a kidney transplant).

THE DIFFERENT PARTS OF MEDICARE:

Medicare Part A (Hospital Insurance) helps cover inpatient care in hospitals. Part A also helps cover skilled nursing facility, hospice, and home health care if you meet certain conditions.

Medicare Part B (Medical Insurance) helps cover medically-necessary services like doctors' services and outpatient care. Part B also helps cover some preventive services to help maintain your health and to keep certain illnesses from getting worse.

Medicare Part C (Medicare Advantage Plans) is another way to get your Medicare benefits. It combines Part A, Part B, and, sometimes, Part D (prescription drug) coverage. Medicare Advantage Plans are managed by private insurance companies approved by Medicare. These plans must cover medically-necessary services. However, plans can charge different copayments, coinsurance, or deductibles for these services.

Medicare Part D (Medicare Prescription Drug Coverage) helps cover prescription drugs. This coverage may help lower your prescription drug costs and help protect against higher costs in the future.

Theories of Aging

The Theory of Programmed Aging is the idea that death is a programmed into the body. The human body is always changing, some cells are lost and some multiply. Basically, the body knows how to repair itself. According to the Theory of Programmed Aging, it would continue to do so indefinitely, unless there was some reason for it to stop which was already programmed into it. For example, one person's liver cells may be programmed to shut off after 72 years, so that a person's liver will stop functioning when they are 72. On the other hand, another person's liver cells may be programmed to stop working after 60 years. This person's liver will stop functioning when they are 60.

Free Radical Theory revolves around cell makeup. An atom's nucleus is surrounded by a cloud of electrons. The electrons are generally in pairs, but sometimes an atom loses an election. When an atom is left with an unpaired electron it is called a free radical, and it can cause damage to a cell. The Free Radical Theory of Aging is that the body continuously produces free radicals, which causes a continuous stream of damage. When enough cells are damaged or killed, it causes aging and eventually death.

The Wear and Tear Theory of Aging is the belief that as time goes on, damage to the body accumulates. Eventually the body's systems just wear out. Examples include liver failure in alcoholics, and lung cancer in smokers. Even regular use can damage the body, such as extended exposure to the sun causing skin cancer.

There are also several other theories of aging:

- Cellular Theory: we only have a certain number of cells, which are programmed to only replicate so many times before they are finished and the body begins to deteriorate.
- Autoimmune Theory: as our bodies age, our immune systems become less effective at fighting disease, stress, etc.
- Genetic Mutation: the number of cells that have problems or mutations that increase with age.

Aging Concerns

Social death is a situation in which a person, who is still living, is excluded from society as if they were dead, or is not treated like an active member of society. This is a situation which sometimes occurs with elderly or terminally ill patients. It can include situations where a person is referred to as if they were already dead, or excluded from conversations.

Osteoporosis is a disorder where the bones are weakened and become porous, like a sponge.

Alzheimer's disease is a chronic condition that deteriorates the nerve fibers in the brain. People with this condition experience memory loss, disorientation and personality changes. Once the disease strikes, the victim's life expectancy is cut in half. Currently, there is little that can be done to treat this condition. The early symptoms of Alzheimer's disease include personality changes, lack of interest in activities, and change in sleep patterns. Alzheimer's disease affects nearly half of all people over 85. It is a condition in which the brain begins to deteriorate in the areas controlling memory, speech, and personality. The early symptoms of Alzheimer's Disease are often confused with depression, another chronic problem for the aging.

Strategies for healthy aging include:

- Developing and maintaining healthy relationships
- Enriching your spiritual life
- Improving physical fitness

Death and Bereavement

Many people fear death. In fact, this is the leading cause of many fears, including fear of public speaking, spiders, heights, confined spaces, etc. There are stages that a person goes through when they find out they have an incurable disease or find out they are going to die. These stages are also known as Kübler-Ross's Stages of Dying, which are:

1. Denial (shock): "This could never happen to me. This must be a mistake."
2. Anger (emotion): "This is unfair. Why me?"
3. Bargaining: "If you don't die, I will do the following…"
4. Preparatory Depression: "There's nothing I can do about this."
5. Acceptance: "I'm ready."

The first stage, denial, consists of the person refusing to acknowledge the fact emotionally, even though they understand intellectually. The statement "I'm too young to die" is an example of someone in this stage.

The second stage, anger, is when the person begins to acknowledge it, and feel powerless, and angry. The statement "How could this happen to me?" could describe a person in this stage.

The third stage is bargaining. In this stage the person wants to compromise. They may want to make a deal with God for more time.

The fourth stage is depression. Withdrawal, sleeping problems or hopelessness can characterize this stage. For a person who has lost a loved one, such as a spouse, they may have an attitude that there is no reason to go on anyway.

The final stage is acceptance. This stage isn't resentful or sullen, but rather passive acceptance of death.

We each deal with death in "our own way", but go through the same stages which are very similar. Here are the stages:

1. Frozen feelings
2. Emotional release
3. Loneliness
4. Physical symptoms
5. Guilt
6. Panic
7. Hostility
8. Selective memory
9. Struggle for new life pattern
10. A feeling that life is good!

Hospice is a system of care for terminally or incurably ill people which is not designed to treat illness, but rather to make the dying process as comfortable as possible once all treatment options have been exhausted. Hospice programs are based on characteristics such as patient and family involvement in care, controlling the symptoms of the patient's illness as much as possible, and round the clock care.

When planning for death, certain issues of business must be attended to. A will, basically one's wishes for the distribution of one's property and possessions after death, should be written and entrusted to the family attorney. This will prevent you from dying intestate, or without a will. This also should be entrusted to family and to an attorney. The person who makes the decisions for your health if you become incapacitated is called a surrogate. It is important to discuss those wishes with your family so that there can be an understanding of your wishes. Organ donation or body donation are other possibilities that you may wish to consider. Discussing your wants for funeral arrangements will help prepare your family for when that day comes. These can be all outlined in a living will.

A living will is a document in which a person outlines what they want to be done as far as medical treatment in the event they become incapacitated. A health proxy on the other hand is a document in which a person states who they want to be making medical decisions for them in the case that they are not able to make them for themselves. The main difference is that a health proxy names another person who makes treatment decisions, and a living will states the patient's wishes. Sometimes a person asks for a DNR (do not resuscitate) order. This means that if the person stops breathing or their heart stops beating then they will not be resuscitated or assisted to live.

Although most people think of burying people when they die, cremation is also a popular process. Cremation is burning dead person's remains, and is usually done in a crematorium. The ashes can then be buried, or kept by the family members. An epitaph are the words written and engraved on a headstone.

ALCOHOL ABUSE

Binge drinking, drinking just to become intoxicated, is becoming more and more problematic. Binge drinking averages at five drinks for a man in a single sitting or four drinks at a sitting.

Alcohol tolerance has to do with the rate at which a person's liver can metabolize alcohol. For the average person, the liver metabolizes alcohol at a rate of about .6 oz (the actual amount of alcohol in about one drink) per hour. However, if a person consistently drinks increased amounts of alcohol, their liver adapts to metabolize it faster by producing more of the necessary enzymes. As a person's alcohol tolerance increases, they have to consume more alcohol for the same effects.

A study published in the British Medical Journal concluded that men who had five drinks a day were more than twice as likely to die from a stroke than non-drinkers. Alcoholism can definitely have an effect on your life expectancy as this condition can also result in cirrhosis of the liver. Alcohol is also now listed as a known carcinogen in the United States.

Ethyl alcohol or ethanol is what makes beer, wine, and liquor intoxicating. There are two main ways to create alcohol. The first is fermentation, where plant sugars are broken down by yeast organisms, creating alcohol and carbon dioxide. This creates a mash. Manufacturers then add other ingredients that dilute the alcohol in the beverage. Other beverages are created with an additional step called distillation – where alcoholic vapors are released from the mash when heated to high temperatures. Proof is the alcohol percentage in the beverage. To figure out the percentage of alcohol in a drink, simply divide the proof by half. For example, 80 proof vodka is 40% alcohol by volume. Most wines are between 12-15% and most beers (depending on state) are between 2-6%.

Acute alcohol intoxication, or alcohol poisoning, occurs when a person has consumed a large amount of alcohol. The main cause of acute alcohol intoxication is binge drinking, or drinking five consecutive drinks in a short amount of time. However, it can also occur if a person consumes household products with alcohol in them. When a person has too much alcohol in the system can depress the nerves controlling involuntary actions such as breathing and the gag reflex. In other words, if a person drinks too much too quickly it can cause a coma, or even death.

Blood-alcohol concentration (BAC) is the ratio of alcohol to the total blood volume. Alcohol is a diuretic, causing increased trips to the bathroom. It also causes dehydration. You also need to be careful of potential drug interaction. Some medications, even over-the-counter, should not be taken with alcohol and vice-versa.

You get the same amount of alcohol whether you drink:

- 1 bottle (12 oz.) beer
- 1 1/5 bottles (14.4 oz.) "light" beer (4% alcohol)
- 1 bottle (12 oz.) of cooler (wine, spirit or beer with around 5% alcohol) 1 glass (3 oz.) sherry
- 1 glass (5 oz.) table wine
- 1 shot (1 ½ oz.) liquor (rye, gin, rum or Scotch)

Long term effects of drinking alcohol include:

- High cholesterol
- Liver disease – the cirrhosis or hardening of the liver
- Alcoholic hepatitis
- Cancer of the throat, stomach, mouth, tongue, breast and liver
- Chronic inflammation of the pancreas

There are many types of treatment programs including:

- Private treatment facilities
- Family, individual and group therapy (Alcoholics Anonymous)
- Drug and aversion therapy (when the drugs you are taking mix with alcohol, headache, nausea, drowsiness and other hangover symptoms appear)

Alcoholism can have many negative consequences for a person. It is unhealthy, and hard on the system. For example, many people who abuse alcohol die of liver failure. Alcoholism also increases the risk of heart disease, certain cancers, and brain damage. Because of this, the life expectancy of alcoholics is about 10-12 years less than the rest of the population.

TOBACCO

Social issues of tobacco include:

- Advertising: Over $14 million dollars in advertising are spent each day. Complaints abound regarding advertising that is directed at teens and children. 90% of all new tobacco users are children and teenagers. Another piece of evidence is that new smokers prefer (86%) one of the three advertised brands, Marlboro, Newport or Camel. Approximately 25% of the population smokes.
- Financial Costs to Society: What is the hidden cost of smoking to society? There is lost productivity, people taking smoke breaks every three hours at work, school, etc. There is also the cost of loss of life because smoking contributes to early death through cancer and other diseases.

OTHER TYPES OF TOBACCO:

- Snuff: A powdered form of tobacco snorted through the nose or held in the mouth between the gum and the cheek.
- Chewing Tobacco: A stringy type of tobacco that is held in the mouth then chewed and sucked.
- Clove Cigarettes: Cigarettes made up of 40% ground cloves and 60% tobacco. Many people mistakenly believe that these cigarettes actually give you a higher dosage of cancer causing chemicals.
- Cigars: Simply tobacco that is wrapped in more tobacco.

Tar is a thick brownish substance, condensed from the matter in smoked tobacco, which forms in the lungs.

Carbon Monoxide is a toxic gas found in cigarette smoke.

Nicotine is the stimulant in tobacco products. It is very powerful and produces a multitude of physiological effects.

TOBACCO FACTS FROM THETRUTH.COM – A PUBLIC TOBACCO AWARENESS ORGANIZATION:

- About 1 out of every 5 deaths in the US can be attributed to tobacco products.
- $72 billion was spent on tobacco-related products by consumers in the U.S. in 1999.
- Every eight seconds, someone in the world dies due to tobacco.
- Every day about 2000 youths become daily smokers.
- Every year cigarettes leave about 31,000 kids fatherless.
- Every day about 4,400 kids age 12 to 17 try a cigarette for the first time.
- Of current smokers in the U.S., 46,000 have lung cancer from smoking.
- In 1999, one year after agreeing to stop billboard advertising, tobacco companies increased advertising spending by 33 percent in magazines with more than 15 percent youth readership.
- In 1990, 72 million bottles of a popular mineral water were voluntarily recalled because of small traces of benzene. The smoke from one pack of unfiltered cigarettes has as much benzene as 169 bottles of the contaminated water.
- How do infants avoid secondhand smoke? "At some point they begin to crawl." — Tobacco Executive 1996
- In as little as 2 weeks, nicotine changes the brain's chemistry and addiction can begin.
- In 2001, tobacco companies spent about $11 billion marketing their products. That's about $1.5 billion more than the year before.
- In 1990, a tobacco company put together a plan to stop Coroners from listing tobacco as a cause of death on a death certificate.

- Cigarette smoke contains 69 chemical compounds that are known to cause cancer.
- There are about 5,412,000 current smokers with a tobacco-related disease in the U.S.
- 1 out of 3 smokers are estimated to eventually die from a tobacco-related disease.
- Of current smokers in the U.S., 1,273,000 have emphysema from smoking.
- Over 50,000 people a year die from secondhand smoke in the US alone.
- Cigarette smoke contains the radioactive isotope Polonium-210.
- In 1989, millions of cases of imported fruit were banned after a small amount of cyanide was found in just two grapes. There's thirty-three times more cyanide in a single cigarette than was found in those two grapes.
- An internal tobacco company marketing report from 1989 said, "We believe that most of the strong, positive images for cigarettes and smoking are created by cinema and television."
- In the mid 90's, a major tobacco company planned on boosting sales of their cigarettes by targeting a new consumer market: gays and homeless people. They called their plan Project Sub-Culture Urban Marketing. Also known as Project SCUM.
- Cigarettes will eventually kill a third of the people who use them.
- Tobacco signage is often placed at a child's eye level.
- One tobacco company developed a genetically-altered tobacco with twice the addictive nicotine of regular tobacco. They code-named it "Y-1."
- In 1984, one tobacco company referred to new customers as "replacement smokers."
- Over 80 percent of all adult smokers started smoking before they turned 18.
- Tobacco companies make $1.8 billion from under age sales.
- Pee contains urea. Some tobacco companies add urea to cigarettes.
- Tobacco companies make a product that kills 440,000 Americans a year.
- Tobacco companies make a product that kills 1,200 Americans a day.
- 2,000 teens start smoking every day.
- Tobacco companies make a product that kills about 50 Americans each hour.
- In the 1970s, tobacco companies started making light cigarettes by putting tiny holes in the filters to let extra air mix with the smoke. They found they could get low readings of toxic agents from FTC-type cigarette testing machines.
- In 1980, a tobacco company considered looking at itself as a "drug company."
- Cigarette smoking is the leading cause of preventable death in the U.S.
- Every 8 seconds, someone in the world dies from tobacco.
- Since 1964, there have been 12 million tobacco-related deaths in the U.S.
- Smoking during pregnancy results in the deaths of about 1000 infants each year in the U.S.
- 70 percent of smokers want to quit. Only about 5 percent actually succeed every year.
- The impact of nicotine is jacked up because tobacco companies add ammonia.

- In the 1980s, tobacco companies started working on making fire-safe cigarettes that would be less likely to ignite furniture or clothing and cause fires. As of 2002, only one of the hundreds of U.S. cigarette brands uses fire safe technology, and cigarettes are still the number one cause of fire-related deaths.
- Every year, 95 percent of people who try to stop smoking are not successful.
- In the US, smoking causes about 445 new cases of lung cancer every day.
- Tobacco kills more Americans than AIDS, drugs, homicides, fires, and auto accidents combined.
- Cigarette smoke contains benzene, carbon monoxide, arsenic, hydrogen cyanide and polonium 210.

Quit Smoking

If you have tried to quit smoking, you know how hard it can be. It is difficult because nicotine is a very addictive drug. For some people, it can be as addictive as heroin or cocaine. Quitting can be hard. Sometimes, people make two or three attempts before finally being able to quit. Each time you try to quit, you can learn about what helps and what hurts.

Quitting takes hard work and a lot of effort, but you can quit smoking.

There are good reasons for quitting. Quitting smoking is one of the most important things you will ever do.

- You will live longer and live better.
- Quitting will lower your chance of having a heart attack, stroke, or cancer.
- If you are pregnant, quitting smoking will improve your chances of having a healthy baby.
- The people you live with, especially your children, will be healthier.
- You will have extra money to spend on things other than cigarettes.

FIVE KEYS FOR QUITTING

Studies have shown that these five steps will help you quit and quit for good. You have the best chances of quitting if you use them together.

1. Get ready.
2. Get support.
3. Learn new skills and behaviors.
4. Get medication and use it correctly.
5. Be prepared for relapse or difficult situations.

1. GET READY

Set a quit date.

Change your environment.

Get rid of ALL cigarettes and ashtrays in your home, car, and place of work.

Don't let people smoke in your home.

Review your past attempts to quit (if any). Think about what worked and what did not.

Once you quit, don't smoke—NOT EVEN A PUFF!

2. GET SUPPORT AND ENCOURAGEMENT

Studies have shown that you have a better chance of being successful if you have help. You can get support in many ways:

Tell your family, friends, and co-workers that you are going to quit and want their support. Ask them not to smoke around you or leave cigarettes out.

Talk to your health care provider (for example, doctor, dentist, nurse, pharmacist, psychologist, or smoking counselor).

Get individual, group, or telephone counseling. The more counseling you have, the better your chances are of quitting. Programs are given at local hospitals and health centers. Call your local health department for information about programs in your area.

3. LEARN NEW SKILLS AND BEHAVIORS

Try to distract yourself from urges to smoke. Talk to someone, go for a walk, or get busy with a task.

When you first try to quit, change your routine. Use a different route to work. Drink tea instead of coffee. Eat breakfast in a different place.

Do something to reduce your stress. Take a hot bath, exercise, or read a book. Plan something enjoyable to do every day.

Drink a lot of water and other fluids.

4. GET MEDICATION AND USE IT CORRECTLY

Medications can help you stop smoking and lessen the urge to smoke.

The U.S. Food and Drug Administration (FDA) has approved five medications to help you quit smoking:

1. Bupropion SR—Available by prescription.
2. Nicotine gum—Available over-the-counter.
3. Nicotine inhaler—Available by prescription.
4. Nicotine nasal spray—Available by prescription.
5. Nicotine patch—Available by prescription and over-the-counter.

Ask your health care provider for advice and carefully read the information on the package.

All of these medications will more or less double your chances of quitting and quitting for good.

Everyone who is trying to quit may benefit from using a medication. If you are pregnant or trying to become pregnant, nursing, under age 18, smoking fewer than 10 cigarettes per day, or have a medical condition, talk to your doctor or other health care provider before taking medications.

5. BE PREPARED FOR RELAPSE OR DIFFICULT SITUATIONS

Most relapses occur within the first three months after quitting. Don't be discouraged if you start smoking again. Remember, most people try several times before they finally quit. Here are some difficult situations to watch for:

Alcohol. Avoid drinking alcohol. Drinking lowers your chances of success.

Other Smokers. Being around those who are smoking can make you want to smoke.

Weight Gain. Many smokers will gain weight when they quit, usually less than 10 pounds. Eat a healthy diet and stay active. Don't let weight gain distract you from your main goal—quitting smoking. Some quit-smoking medications may help delay weight gain.

Bad Mood or Depression. There are a lot of ways to improve your mood other than smoking.

If you are having problems with any of these situations, talk to your doctor or other health care provider.

SPECIAL SITUATIONS OR CONDITIONS

Studies suggest that everyone can quit smoking. Your situation or condition can give you a special reason to quit.

- Pregnant women/new mothers. By quitting, you protect your baby's health and your own.
- Hospitalized patients. By quitting, you reduce health problems and help healing.
- Heart attack patients. By quitting, you reduce your risk of a second heart attack.
- Lung, head, and neck cancer patients. By quitting, you reduce your chance of a second cancer.
- Parents of children and adolescents. By quitting, you protect your children and adolescents from illnesses caused by second-hand smoke.

QUESTIONS TO THINK ABOUT

Think about the following questions before you try to stop smoking. You may want to talk about your answers with your health care provider.

1. Why do you want to quit?
2. When you tried to quit in the past, what helped and what didn't?
3. What will be the most difficult situations for you after you quit? How will you plan to handle them?
4. Who can help you through the tough times? Your family? Friends? Health care provider?
5. What pleasures do you get from smoking? What ways can you still get pleasure if you quit?

HERE ARE SOME QUESTIONS TO ASK YOUR HEALTH CARE PROVIDER

1. How can you help me to be successful at quitting?
2. What medication do you think would be best for me and how should I take it?
3. What should I do if I need more help?
4. What is smoking withdrawal like? How can I get information on withdrawal?

Illicit Drugs

Not all drugs are considered illicit or illegal drugs. Over-the-counter drugs, also known as OTC, are drugs that can be purchased without a prescription. These include drugs that are considered "safe" for general use and include items such as anti-histamines, sedatives, anti-fungal, and pain medication. More powerful opiates such as codeine, heroin, opium, and methadone are not available without a prescription from a doctor and must be picked up with identification. These items are considered illegal without a prescription. Some of these items can be abuse with or without a prescription. If you do not have a prescription for the drug yourself, then the drug is considered illegal or illicit for your consumption.

Cocaine or coke is a powerful stimulant made from the leaves of the South American coca shrub. Freebase is the most powerful distillate of cocaine. Crack is cocaine that comes in rocks or chips.

Marijuana is usually smoked as a cigarette or joint, or in a pipe or bong, although marijuana has appeared in "blunts" in recent years. These are cigars that have been emptied of tobacco and re-filled with marijuana, sometimes in combination with another drug, such as crack. Some users also mix marijuana into foods or use it to brew tea.

The main active chemical in marijuana is THC (delta-9-tetrahydrocannabinol). Short-term effects of marijuana use include problems with memory and learning; distorted perception; difficulty in thinking and problem-solving; loss of coordination; and increased heart rate, anxiety, and panic attacks.

Heroin

Years ago, thoughts of using a needle kept many potential heroin users at bay. Not anymore. Today's heroin is so pure that users can smoke it or snort it, causing more kids under 18 to use it. Kids who snort or smoke heroin face the same high risk of overdose and death that haunts intravenous users. Yet 40% of high school seniors polled do not believe there is great risk in trying heroin.

Recent studies suggest a shift from injecting to snorting or smoking heroin because of increased purity and the misconception that these forms of use will not lead to addiction.

Heroin is processed from morphine, a naturally occurring substance extracted from the seed-pod of the Asian poppy plant. Heroin usually appears as a white or brown powder. Street names associated with heroin include smack, H, skag, and junk. Other names may refer to types of heroin produced in a specific geographical area, such as Mexican black tar.

The short-term effects of heroin abuse appear soon after a single dose and disappear in a few hours. After an injection of heroin, the user reports feeling a surge of euphoria (a "rush") accompanied by a warm flushing of the skin, a dry mouth, and heavy extremities. Following this initial euphoria, the user goes "on the nod," an alternately wakeful and drowsy state. Mental functioning becomes clouded due to the depression of the central nervous system.

Inhalants

Inhalants are common products found right in the home and are among the most popular and deadly substances kids abuse. Inhalant abuse can result in death from the very first use. About one in five kids report having used inhalants by the eighth grade. Teens use inhalants by sniffing or "snorting" fumes from containers; spraying aerosols directly into the mouth or nose; bagging, by inhaling a substance inside a paper or plastic bag; huffing from an inhalant-soaked rag; or inhaling from balloons filled with nitrous oxide.

Inhalants are breathable chemical vapors that produce psychoactive (mind-altering) effects. Although people are exposed to volatile solvents and other inhalants in the home and in the workplace, many do not think of "inhalable" substances as drugs because most of them were never meant to be used in that way.

Young people are likely to abuse inhalants, in part, because inhalants are readily available and inexpensive. Parents should see that these substances are monitored closely so that children do not abuse them.

Ecstasy

MDMA, short for methylenedioxymethamphetamine, called "Adam", "ecstasy", or "XTC" on the street, is a synthetic, psychoactive (mind-altering) drug with hallucinogenic and amphetamine-like properties. Its chemical structure is similar to two other synthetic drugs, MDA and methamphetamine, which are known to cause brain damage.

Beliefs about MDMA are reminiscent of similar claims made about LSD in the 1950s and 1960s, which proved to be untrue. According to its proponents, MDMA can make people trust each other and can break down barriers between therapists and patients, lovers, and family members.

LSD

LSD, aka "acid", is odorless, colorless, and has a slightly bitter taste and is usually taken by mouth. Often LSD is added to absorbent paper, such as blotter paper, and divided into small, decorated squares, with each square representing one dose.

Physical Psychological short-term effects. The effects of LSD are unpredictable. They depend on the amount taken; the user's personality, mood, and expectations; and the surroundings in which the drug is used. Usually, the user feels the first effects of the drug 30 to 90 minutes after taking it. The physical effects include dilated pupils, higher body temperature, increased heart rate and blood pressure, sweating, loss of appetite, sleeplessness, dry mouth, and tremors.

Sensations and feelings change much more dramatically than the physical signs. The user may feel several different emotions at once or swing rapidly from one emotion to another. If taken in a large enough dose, the drug produces delusions and visual hallucinations. The user's sense of time and self changes. Sensations may seem to "cross over", giving the user the feeling of hearing colors and seeing sounds. These changes can be frightening and can cause panic.

LSD trips are long typically they begin to clear after about 12 hours. Some users experience severe, terrifying thoughts and feelings, fear of losing control, fear of insanity and death, and despair while using LSD. In some cases, fatal accidents have occurred during states of LSD intoxication.

Flashbacks. Many LSD users experience flashbacks, recurrence of certain aspects of a person's experience, without the user having taken the drug again. A flashback occurs suddenly, often without warning, and may occur within a few days or more than a year after LSD use. Flashbacks usually occur in people who use hallucinogens chronically or have an underlying personality problem; however, otherwise healthy people who use LSD occasionally may also have flashbacks. Bad trips and flashbacks are only part of the risks of LSD use. LSD users may manifest relatively long-lasting psychoses, such as schizophrenia or severe depression. It is difficult to determine the extent and mechanism of the LSD involvement in these illnesses.

Peyote and Mescaline

Peyote is a small, spineless cactus, Lophophora williamsii, whose principal active ingredient is the hallucinogen mescaline (3, 4, 5-trimethoxyphenethylamine). From earliest recorded time, peyote has been used by natives in northern Mexico and the southwestern United States as a part of their religious rites.

The top of the cactus above ground--also referred to as the crown--consists of disc-shaped buttons that are cut from the roots and dried. These buttons are generally chewed or soaked in water to produce an intoxicating liquid. The hallucinogenic dose of mescaline is about 0.3 to 0.5 grams and lasts about 12 hours. While peyote produced rich visual hallucinations that were important to the native American peyote users, the full spectrum of effects served as a chemically induced model of mental illness. Mescaline can be extracted from peyote or produced synthetically. Both peyote and mescaline are listed in the CSA as Schedule I hallucinogens.

Steroids

Anabolic steroids are a group of powerful compounds that are synthetic derivatives of the male sex hormone testosterone. These drugs are used illegally by body builders, long-distance runners, cyclists and various other athletes who claim steroids give them a competitive advantage and/or improve their physical performance. Taken in combination with a program of muscle-building exercise and diet, steroids may contribute to increases in body weight and muscular strength. Approximately 2% of teenagers will use steroids before they graduate from high school.

Physical Fitness

The President's Council on Physical Fitness and Sports was created to address the concerns of low fitness levels of American children. Their aim is to "promote, encourage and motivate Americans of all ages to become physically active and participate in sports." It is each person's personal responsibility through their actions to maintain proper fitness and health through diet and exercise.

Another part of physical fitness is ensuring that you receive the proper amount of exercise. There are two main types of exercise which are isokinetic and isotonic. Isokinetic exercises are exercises that use a machine to control the exact amount of the speed of the muscle contraction. Isotonic exercises are where your muscle contracts, but your joints don't move and the muscle fibers stay at the same length. These types of exercises are used for developing strength and rehabilitation for muscles.

Systolic blood pressure: the pressure in the arteries during a heartbeat; not regular if over 160 mm Hg or above. Diastolic blood pressure: abnormal if consistently 95 mm Hg or above.

Lipids are fats that circulate in the bloodstream and are stored in your body. Regular exercise is known to reduce the levels of low-density lipoproteins.

LDLs: bad cholesterol

HDLs: good cholesterol

Cholesterol is a type of fat which circulates through the blood stream. There are two different types of cholesterol. There are High Density Lipoproteins (HDL) and Low Density Lipoproteins (LDL). Low Density Lipoproteins (LDL) are considered "bad cholesterol" because they transport fat to the body's cells. Also LDL can accumulate on the walls of arteries and become a health risk. On the other hand, HDL is considered "good cholesterol" because it is used to transport cholesterol to the liver for metabolism, when it will be eliminated from the body.

Most people desire to start a physical fitness plan because they want to lose weight. Exercise also helps prevent diabetes, increases longevity, improves the immune system, improves mental health and stress management, improves skeletal mass, and improves physical fitness. Another benefit of exercise is increased memory, especially in older adults. This is due to the increase of oxygen rich blood to the brain, lower blood sugar levels and the endorphins released during exercise.

An aerobic exercise program improves cardiorespiratory fitness. Exercise frequency begins at three days a week and moves up to five. Exercise intensity involves working out at your target heart rate. Exercise duration should increase to 30 to 45 minutes; the longer the period, the more calories burned.

Regular exercise has many positive effects. It can be an antidepressant, decreases chances of getting certain diseases, and releases endorphins, a hormone which makes people happy. Among the positive effects of exercise is its effect on learning ability. Although it was previously believed that it wasn't possible to grow new neurons, recent studies have shown that exercise may increase neuron production. Specifically, the benefits seem to be directed at the hippocampus, the memory section of the brain.

Heart Rate

It is important to know your resting and target heart rate. Your resting heart rate is when your heart is at rest. The best time to find it is first thing in the morning before you get up and moving for the day. Count the times your heart beats for one full minute. The heart beats about 60 to 80 times per minute while at rest. To figure out your target heart rate, you must first calculate your high and low end of your target heart rate zone.

To calculate the low end of your target heart rate zone which is about 50% of your heart rate reserve, use the following formula:

220 - (your age) = Max Heart Rate (MaxHR)
MaxHR - (resting heart rate) = Heart Rate Reserve (HRR)
HRR x 50% = training range %
training range % + resting heart rate = low end of target heart rate zone

The following example shows the low end of a target heart rate for a 37-year-old person with a resting heart rate of 62 bpm:

220 - 37 = 183
185 - 60 = 121
121 x 50%= 60.5
60.5 + 62 = 122.5 beats per minute

To find the high end of the zone, use the following formula:

220 - (your age) = Max Heart Rate (MaxHR)
MaxHR - (resting heart rate) = Heart Rate Reserve (HRR)
HRR x 85% = training range %
training range % + RHR = high end of your target heart rate

Now you know the range which you need to stay within for optimal exercise.

Platelets in Blood

Platelets are small cell fragments in the blood. Their main function is to stop bleeding, by forming clots. For example, platelets come into play when a person gets a cut. The platelets gather together around the cut area, stopping blood flow, and forming a scab. The ideal amount of platelets in the blood is 150 thousand to 450 thousand platelets per micro liter of blood. When there are too many or too few platelets in the blood, it can cause problems. For example, if there are too many platelets the blood can clot when it shouldn't. If this were to happen in the brain it would cause a stroke. If there are too few platelets, then scabs won't form over cuts. In addition to increased blood loss, this would also create increased risk of infection.

Muscle Movement & Flexibility

Flexibility exercises should be performed in sets of four or more repetitions and done at least two or three days a week for performance to hold.

There are three principles of strength development:

- Tension Principle: The more tension you create in a muscle, the greater your strength will be. The most common way this is done is by lifting weights.

- Overload Principle: Setting a base level for your strength then overloading your muscle by causing it to perform at a level exceeding what it is accustomed to doing.
- Specificity of Training Principle: If you only work your legs, only your legs will see the benefit of exercise.

There are three types of muscle action:

- Isometric: force produced without any joint movement
- Concentric: force produced while the muscle is shortening
- Eccentric: force produced while the muscle is lengthening

Hypertrophy is the increased size (girth) of a muscle.

Methods of resistance:

- Body weight resistance: Using body weight as resistance (instead of weights) during exercise.
- Fixed Resistance: Barbells or dumbbells used for exercise. Referred to as "fixed" because their weights are set and do not change.
- Variable Resistance: Gives muscles exercise through a full range of motion. A home version, for example, includes resistance bands.
- Accommodating Resistance: Resistance changes according to the amount of force generated.

Aerobic exercise: any type of exercise usually performed for 20 to 30 minutes or longer.

Headache

A headache is a common malady. There are many different types of headache which include:

- Tension headache. A tension headache can be episodic or chronic. Generally caused by a temporary stress, anxiety or fear and can be treated with over the counter medication.
- Migraine headache. This type of headache is the most debilitating and results in the most job absenteeism than any other headache type. This headache generally occurs on one side of the head where blood vessels around the brain are inflamed and give off pain signals.

- Cluster headaches. This type of headache can occur several times a day. The word cluster refers to the amount of rescission that takes place. A cluster headache can be the most painful but lasts only 30 to 45 minutes. However, it can and will reoccur several times during the day.
- Hormone headache. Hormone headaches are those that are triggered by hormones, such as a women's menstrual cycle.

Headaches can be treated with OTC medicines. However, some repeat sufferers have prescribed pain medications to help relieve the pain.

Nutrition

The science of the relationship between body function and the essential elements we eat. Calorie is a measure of energy we obtain from a particular food. The food pyramid includes the following:

- Breads, Cereals, Rice and Pasta Group (6-11 servings)
- Fruit Group (2-4 servings)
- Vegetable Group (3-5 servings)
- Meat, Poultry, Fish, Dry Beans, Eggs and Nuts Group (2-3 servings)
- Milk, Yogurt, and Cheese (2 servings; 3 servings for pregnant or breast feeding women)
- Fats, Oils, Sweets (use sparingly)

Correct serving portions are important, especially to maintain a specific weight. For example, one portion of meat is equal to a deck of cards. Each slice of bread, waffle, tortilla is one serving of bread. One cup of milk is also a serving.

The following lists parts of the body and their role in nutrition:

- Esophagus: The tube that transports food from the mouth to the stomach. Step 1 in digestion.
- Stomach: A large muscular organ that temporarily stores, mixes, and digests food. Step 2 in digestion.
- Small intestine: A 20 ft coiled tube. The final part of digestion.

Dehydration is the depletion of body fluids, a result from lack of water. The human body is 50-60% water. A normal healthy body maintains a body temperature of about 98.6 degrees Fahrenheit.

The ability to regulate body temperature is called homeostasis. Water helps regulate body temperature. When you exercise, you lose water through sweat and your breath. If the body does not have the ability to sweat, it will not be able to cool itself. Paraplegics may not have the ability to sweat because of injury to their spinal cord and therefore must be very careful of their body's temperature.

Protein

After water, protein is the most abundant substance in the body. Proteins are necessary for development and repair of blood, bones, muscle and skin. Proteins also transport nutrients to all of the body's cells. When proteins are consumed they are broken down into smaller molecules called amino acids.

Proteins are often called the "building blocks of life" because protein is used in growth and repair. Amino acids are the "building blocks of proteins." There are 20 amino acids that the human body needs to properly function, and of that 20 the body naturally produces 11. The remaining nine are called essential amino acids, and are gained through what a person eats. If a food has all nine of these amino acids, it is called a complete protein. Complete proteins naturally occur in animal protein, such as meat and dairy products. However, animal proteins are not the only way to obtain complex protein. Plants produce incomplete proteins, and the body can build complete proteins by combining incomplete proteins. Because of this it is possible for a vegetarian to obtain the necessary amounts of protein.

There are three categories of plant produced proteins, or incomplete proteins. The first is grains, such as pasta or whole grain products. The second is legumes, like beans and soy products. The third is seeds and nuts. When you mix foods from these categories you can create a complete protein. One combination that is quite common is a peanut butter sandwich.

We need these essential amino acids in order to survive so they must be consumed through food or dietary supplement. Carbohydrates are basic nutrients that give the body energy to sustain normal activity. Simple sugars are a major type of carbohydrate, which provide short-term energy. Complex carbohydrates are a major type of carbohydrate, which provide sustained, longer lasting energy.

There is a myth about sugar consumption and hyperactivity – recent studies show no links between hyperactive behavior and sugar.

The body converts all types of simple sugars into glucose. In its natural form, glucose is sweet, and comes from substances such as corn syrup, honey, molasses, vegetables, and fruits.

Fructose is another simple sugar found in fruits and berries. Glucose and fructose are monosaccharides and contain only one molecule of sugar. Disaccharides are combinations of two monosaccharides. The most common disaccharide is table sugar. Polysaccharides are complex carbohydrates formed by the combining of long chains of saccharides. There are two major types of complex carbohydrates: starches and fiber or cellulose.

Fiber is an important part of diet. Fiber is the digestible part of plants that helps move foods through the digestive system. Fiber also helps prevent colon and rectal cancer, breast cancer, diabetes, heart disease, obesity, and constipation. Good examples of fiber are lettuce and apples.

Fats are the basic nutrients composed or carbon and hydrogen atoms; needed for the proper functioning of cells and insulating body organs, fats help regulate body temperature, and aid in creating healthy skin and hair. Fats also have more calories than carbohydrates or protein.

Triglyceride is the most common form of fat in the body; excess calories that are consumed are converted into triglycerides and are stored as fat.

Cholesterol is a form of fat circulating in the blood that can accumulate on the inner walls of arteries.

Saturated fats are solid at room temperature and derived from animal sources. Unsaturated fats are derived from plants, liquid at room temperature. There are many different kinds of fats, and they all have different effects on the body. It's more important to pay attention to what kinds of fats are being consumed, than how much fat is being consumed. Trans-fat is often considered one of the worst types of fats, because it has the effect of heightening a person's LDL (bad cholesterol) and lowering their HDL (good cholesterol). Trans-fats are more solid than oil is, and because of this it is often used to make foods feel less greasy, and so that they will last longer.

Anemia is an iron deficiency that results from the body's inability to produce hemoglobin. Folate is a type of vitamin B. In 1998 the FDA mandated folate fortification in all bread, cereal, rice and macaroni sold in the U.S. This practice will boost most people's intake of vitamin B as well as prevent spina bifida and other birth defects.

Types of vegetarians:

- Vegans: eat no foods of animal origin
- Lacto-Vegetarians: avoid flesh foods but eat dairy
- Ovo-Vegetarians: avoid flesh foods but eat eggs
- Lacto-Ovo-Vegetarians: avoid flesh foods but eat both dairy and eggs
- Pesco-Vegetarians: avoid: meat but eat fish, dairy products and eggs
- Semi-Vegetarians: eat chicken, fish, dairy and eggs

Food irradiation is when food is treated with gamma radiation from radioactive x-rays to kill microorganisms. Organically grown foods are grown without the use of pesticides and chemicals.

Obesity and Weight Loss

Obesity is a weight disorder that is defined as an accumulation of fat determined beyond normal by age, body type, etc. Body mass index or BMI is figured as follows:

BMI = Weight (in lbs.) / 2.2 (Height (in inches) / 39.4)2

The BMI of a healthy person is 19-25.

Another way to determine body fat is called hydrostatic weighing, which is where a person is submerged in water and the amount of water that is displaced is measured and tracked.

Waist-to-hip ratio is another way to measure fat distribution. Excess fat in the abdominal area poses a greater health risk than fat in the hips and thighs. Women primarily store fat in the hips, buttocks and thighs. Men store fat in the upper body, mostly the upper area and stomach.

Most people should eat a maximum of 2000 calories a day, give or take, based on their activity level. Satiety is the feeling of fullness or satisfaction at the end of the meal. Plateau is the point in a weight-loss program at which the dieter finds it difficult to lose more weight. The Setpoint theory suggests that the body acts in a way to keep a specific amount of body fat.

Even while at rest, the body consumes energy. About 70% of the energy that a person consumes in a day is used without them having to do anything. The basal metabolic rate or BMR is the term for the amount of energy expended while at rest. This value can fluctuate, for example, the younger a person is the higher their BMR tends to be. When keeping in mind that 3500 calories equals 1 pound (lb.) of body weight, it is easier to make food choices.

Eating disorders include:

- Anorexia nervosa: self-starvation
- Bulimia: binge and purge (eat a lot then throw up so you don't gain weight)

Because of poverty and hunger, the school lunch system was started so that all children could get at least one "square" meal a day. Protein deficiency is generally found within lower class families.

Immunizations

Immunization is the process by which a person becomes immune to a disease. There are two types of immunization, passive and active. In passive immunization, already made antibodies are transferred to another person. This method isn't always the most useful because antibodies are programmed to die within a short amount of time, making it a temporary solution. However, it can be useful if a person is already sick, and for some reason cannot produce their own antibodies. Active immunization is when the antigen is directly introduced into a system. Active immunization is permanent. Once a person is actively immunized they will be protected from the disease for the rest of their lives. This can happen naturally, such as when a person gets sick, or it can happen through methods such as vaccination. Vaccination is when a person is immunized against a disease by having killed or weakened pathogens introduced into their system. In this way their body learns how to fight the disease without risk of being seriously sickened or disabled by it.

There are vaccines for many different diseases. The vaccines for chickenpox, measles, mumps, polio, and whooping cough are among those that are recommended in the United States. The first vaccine was the smallpox vaccine. Smallpox is believed to have killed over 300 million people in the 1900s alone. It was so dangerous that it was even used as a type of biological weapon in the 1700s during the French and Indian War. Smallpox infected blankets were distributed to native peoples, and the disease decimated their populations. In 1796, Edward Jenner, a British physician, developed the vaccine, and since that time it is believed to have been completely eliminated from natural occurrence. In other words, although some strains exist in laboratories, it isn't naturally occurring anymore.

Polio is another disease which a vaccine has been developed for. Polio is a disease which can enter the body through the nose or mouth, and makes its way to the central nervous system. Polio can only grow in live cells, so once it's in the central nervous system, it enters a cell and begins to multiply, which eventually kills the cell. If enough cells are killed, it can cause paralysis, or in some cases death. The vaccine was introduced in 1955, and was developed by Jonas E. Salk. Since that time cases have become rare. With polio, the vaccine is very important because so far no way has been discovered to treat it once it is already inside the body.

TYPES OF INFECTIONS

There are two types of infections:

- Staphylococci infection: an organism that lives on the skin and when it enters the skin causes an infection
- Streptococcal infection: includes strep throat, Scarlet fever, rheumatic fever

Strep throat is very contagious between anyone with close contact. If not treated, you can have secondary complications such as rheumatic fever which can damage for heart permanently, leaving you susceptible to future problems. Strep throat can be diagnosed by a family physician which a culture test and is treated with antibiotics.

Other infections:

- Pneumonia: disease of the lungs
- Legionnaire's Disease: famous from a 1976 outbreak when several Legionnaires at the American Legion convention contracted the disease and died before the organism could be isolated.
- Tuberculosis (TB): also known as white death. Patients are quarantined and treated with drugs.
- Mononucleosis: also known as the kissing disease, which results in sore throat, chills, body weakness, fever, nausea, etc. It is NOT as contagious as the common cold.

Stages of Infections

An infectious disease is classified as an illness that is caused by a pathogen. Infectious diseases tend to follow the same patterns, though the specific symptoms may vary.

The first stage of infection is the incubation period. During this period, the person might not even be aware that they are sick, and if the immune system is successful the person may never realize that they had an infection. This stage takes different amounts of time for different diseases.

For example, the incubation period for the common cold is only a day or so, whereas the incubation period for chickenpox is 2-3 weeks. After the incubation period is the prodromal period. This is when the first signs of sickness begin to appear, such as general fatigue or low fever. Again, if the immune system is successful the sickness could stop after this point. The third stage of infectious disease is the invasive phase, or the illness stage.

This is when specific symptoms begin to emerge, and the immune system does everything it can to stop the infection. Assuming it is successful, the person would be in the final stage. This is called the convalescence period. In this stage the person gets health again, and the body begins to repair damage caused by the infection. This stage lasts different lengths depending on the severity of the disease.

Hepatitis

Hepatitis is the inflammation of the liver. It also has a variety of other symptoms. There are three types of Hepatitis:

- Hepatitis A: contracted from a fecal-oral route
- Hepatitis B: contracted through bodily fluids
- Hepatitis C: previous to 1992, contracted through organ transplants and blood transfusions

There are vaccines for Hepatitis A & B, but not for C. Treatments for A and B have been very successful, unlike treatments for C.

Epidemics and Pandemics

Epidemic and pandemic are two very nearly interchangeable words. The biggest difference between the two is scale. An epidemic is when a disease spreads far above the expected infection rate for a specific group of people in a specific place. For example, if the amount of people expected to get a disease in a specific city is 15%, it would be an epidemic if 50% of the people got sick. With a pandemic, the scale is much bigger. A pandemic is when a disease spreads much faster than expected over a large area. Generally, the word pandemic is used to refer to global spread. An example of a pandemic is the Black Plague, or Bubonic Plague, which spread across all of Europe and killed millions of people in the 1300s.

Pathogens

A pathogen is an organism which causes disease. Pathogens can be found almost anywhere. Some spread through food, such as E. coli. Other pathogens spread through air or physical contact, like the flu. A pathogen can be anything from bacteria, to virus, to fungi. Bacteria are single celled organisms, and are one form of pathogen. For example, Tuberculosis is a disease caused by bacteria. A virus is another type of pathogen. The chickenpox, measles, and mumps are all examples of diseases caused by a virus. Fungi can also be pathogens, and are responsible for diseases like athlete's foot and ringworm.

T-Cells

Active immunity is how the body fights diseases with antibodies that it produces. These cells are used to combat antigens. Antigens are anything which triggers a response from the immune system. Thousands of different types of B cells are produced every day in the bone marrow, and are designed to detect certain antigens. Once a B cell finds its particular antigen, the T cells kick in. There are several different types of T cells. Helper T cells are activated when the B cell finds its antigen. Their job is to tell the B cells to produce antibodies, and to activate the cytotoxic T cells. Cytotoxic T cells or "killer T cells" attack the antigen. One of the most important functions of the immune system is to determine what in the body should be attacked and what should not. Suppressor T cells stop the immune system from attacking something that is part of the body. In other words, it suppresses the activity of B cells and Cytotoxic T Cells. Once the body has learned how to defeat a specific antigen it creates memory B and T cells. These cells have long lives, and their job is to remember how to defeat that antigen in case it is ever present again. This is why some diseases can only be caught once, such as chickenpox. Once a person has had it, the memory cells know how to defeat it if it sees it again.

Human Immunodeficiency Virus or HIV is a disease which helps show why helper T cells are so important to the immune system. HIV attacks the helper T cells, which are what activate cytotoxic T cells, and signal the B cells to make antibodies. When there isn't a sufficient number of helper T cells, the immune system has a much more difficult time fighting infections.

Measles

Measles (also known as Rubeola) is a significant contagious infectious disease caused by a virus. Fortunately, measles is less common in the United States and other developed countries because an effective vaccine became available in 1963. Measles begins as a respiratory ailment evident as nasal blocking, sore throat, and red and/or watery eyes. In addition, measles is evident by a high fever of at least three days' duration and the existence of the three Cs: Cough, Coryza (runny nose), and Conjunctivitis (red eyes). The contagion period lasts for 4-12 days during which there are no symptoms. Infected people are contagious from the appearance of the first symptoms until 3-5 days after the rash appears.

Like chickenpox, measles is caused by a virus. In some cases, sores first appear in the mouth; these are called Koplik's sores. These sores are very transient and are not often seen. Measles can be spread through direct contact or from a cough or sneeze.

A common form of measles is called rubella (also known as German measles or three-day measles). Many cases of rubella are mild and may be misdiagnosed or are so mild they go undetected. Most people who have measles with no complications, recover with rest and any supportive treatment given. Complications from measles are rare and range from diarrhea to pneumonia and encephalitis. It is recommended that babies be inoculated 6 to 8 months after birth, with a booster shot at 4 to 5 years of age. Babies are generally immune for the first few months of life due to an immunity passed on from their mothers.

What preventative measures should be taken? The answer is the same—vaccinations. Children who were not inoculated in their early months should be inoculated by age 11 or 12. Measles inoculations are a series, and many young people may have started the series but never completed it. Should adults be inoculated? Absolutely! Having the disease can be much worse than having the "shots!" German measles is a milder version of the disease.

Mumps

Mumps is a viral infection, causing a painful enlargement of the salivary glands. These glands are located within your cheek near your jaw bone. Mumps can also cause painful swelling of other glands, especially in adults. About 20 percent of adult males have some swelling of the testicular glands. Sterility is rarely a result, and hormonal activity returns.

The mumps virus lodges in the upper respiratory tract. The virus is transmitted through respiratory secretions or saliva, such as coughing or sneezing. Exposure to an infected person puts you at the risk of developing mumps.

What are some of the symptoms? Symptoms include fever, chilly sensations, headache, stiff, aching muscles, and loss of appetite. The onset of these symptoms typically occurs 14 to 24 days after exposure to the virus.

The patient should be isolated until the glandular swelling has subsided. Contacts with others should be limited for 14 to 28 days after the onset.

What precautions should you take during the period of incubation? Currently, there is no one treatment for mumps. Rather, the treatment should correspond to the symptom. For example, if the patient has difficulty swallowing, feed him/her a soft diet. Avoid acidic drinks (fruit juices), as these may irritate the throat.

What other preventative steps can be taken? Be sure you have current inoculations. The MMR (measles, mumps, and rubella) vaccine is recommended. Then, avoid contact with infected persons. Wash your hands often and always before eating and after using the bathroom.

Mumps were very common until 1968. That year, a vaccine was developed and became available to all households and the incidence for the disease dropped. This is a dangerous disease that for young men has the potential of causing sterility and both genders risk hearing loss. This is one of the vaccines that is required for public school admissions.

In summary, you have learned that these three common infectious diseases, chickenpox, measles and mumps have many similarities. Each is caused by a virus, so antibiotics are ineffective. All three are highly contagious, so the treatment process will be similar. Minimize your contact with the infected person. If the infected person is a child, keep other children away from contact. Wear gloves and a mask when you must touch the infected person. Make sure you and your family are vaccinated, and maintain a permanent record of when the vaccinations are given.

Viral Diseases & Vocabulary

Rabies is a viral disease which is contracted through animal bites. Bats are carriers of this disease. Because they are symptom free, they are called asymptomatic. Their urine contains the virus, making a trip into an even mildly populated cave unwise, putting you at a risk to contract it through the air. The disease can be fatal if not treated immediately. Anyone bitten by an animal that may have rabies should get medical attention immediately and if possible, have the animal tested.

Fungi includes the mold on bread and cheese. This type of fungi causes humans no harm. However, other types of fungi, including Candidiasis (vaginal yeast infection), athlete's foot, jock itch and ringworm, are fungal diseases. Keep the affected area clean and dry in addition to taking the medication prescribed.

Protozoa are microscopic single-celled organisms that are associated with tropical diseases such as malaria and giardiasis. To prevent the spread of these diseases, water sources must be purified and treated.

Vocabulary:

Pathogen: a disease-causing agent
Epidemic: an outbreak of a disease that affects many people in an entire community
Pandemics: a global epidemic of disease
Virulent: how aggressive a pathogen is in creating disease
Sickle Cell Anemia: a genetic disease that is commonly found among African Americans

Bacteria

Bacteria is a single celled organism that may be disease-causing. Bacteria and viruses are sometimes confused. A virus cannot live without a host. Bacteria is 99% of the time helpful to humans. Viruses serve no useful purpose. Bacteria is considered alive while viruses are not considered living creatures and cannot be killed in the same way as antibiotics do with bacteria.

Sexually Transmitted Diseases

Sexually transmitted diseases (STDs) affect men and women of all backgrounds and economic levels. Despite the fact that a great deal of progress has been made in STD prevention over the past four decades, the United States has the highest rates of STDs in the industrialized world. The rates of STDs are 50-100 times higher in the U.S. than in other industrial nations, even though rates of gonorrhea and syphilis have recently been brought to historic lows. In the United States alone, an estimated 15.3 million new cases of STDs are reported each year.

Despite the fact that STDs are extremely widespread and add billions of dollars to the nation's healthcare costs each year, most people in the United States remain unaware of the risk and consequences of all but the most prominent STD—HIV, the virus that causes AIDS.

COMMON STDS AND THE ORGANISMS THAT CAUSE THEM

Many people are aware of the most prominent STD—HIV. However, many other STDs affect millions of men and women each year. Many of these STDs initially cause no symptoms, especially in women. Symptoms, when they do develop, may be confused with those of other diseases that are not transmitted through sexual contact. STDs can still be transmitted person to person even if they do not show symptoms.

Also, health problems caused by STDs tend to be more severe for women than for men.

Below are descriptions of several of the most common STDs, including information about incidence, symptoms (if any), and treatment.

ACQUIRED IMMUNE DEFICIENCY SYNDROME (AIDS)

AIDS (acquired immunodeficiency syndrome) was first reported in the United States in 1981. It is caused by the human immunodeficiency virus (HIV), a virus that destroys the body's ability to fight off infection.

An estimated 900,000 people in the United States are currently infected with HIV. People who have AIDS are very susceptible to many life-threatening diseases, called opportunistic infections, and to certain forms of cancer. Transmission of the virus primarily occurs during sexual activity and by sharing needles used to inject intravenous drugs.

CHANCROID

Chancroid ("SHAN-kroid") is an important bacterial infection caused by Haemophilus ducreyi, which is spread by sexual contact. Periodic outbreaks of chancroid have occurred in the United States, the last one being in the late 1980s. These outbreaks are usually seen in minority populations in the inner cities, especially in the southern and eastern portion of the country. Globally, this disease is common in sub-Saharan Africa among men who have frequent contact with prostitutes.

The infection begins with the appearance of painful open sores on the genitals, sometimes accompanied by swollen, tender lymph nodes in the groin. These symptoms occur within a week after exposure. Symptoms in women are often less noticeable and may be limited to painful urination or defecation, painful intercourse, rectal bleeding, or vaginal discharge. Chancroid lesions may be difficult to distinguish from ulcers caused by genital herpes or syphilis. A physician must therefore diagnose the infection by excluding other diseases with similar symptoms. People with chancroid can be treated effectively with one of several antibiotics. Chancroid is one of the genital ulcer diseases that may be associated with an increased risk of transmission of the human immunodeficiency virus (HIV), the cause of AIDS.

CHLAMYDIA

Chlamydial ("kla-MID-ee-uhl") infection is the most common bacterial sexually transmitted disease (STD) in the United States today. The U.S. Center for Disease Control and Prevention estimates that more than 4 million new cases occur each year. The highest rates of chlamydial infection are in 15- to 19-year-old adolescents regardless of demographics or location.

Chlamydial infection is caused by a bacterium, Chlamydia trachomatis, and can be transmitted during vaginal, oral, or anal sexual contact with an infected partner. A pregnant woman may pass the infection to her newborn during delivery, with subsequent neonatal eye infection or pneumonia.

Pelvic inflammatory disease (PID), a serious complication of chlamydial infection, has emerged as a major cause of infertility among women of childbearing age. The annual cost of chlamydial infection is estimated to exceed $2 billion.

GENITAL HERPES/HSV

Genital herpes is a contagious viral infection that affects an estimated one out of four (or 45 million) Americans. Doctors estimate that as many as 500,000 new cases may occur each year. The infection is caused by the herpes simplex virus (HSV). There are two types of HSV, and both can cause genital herpes. HSV type 1 most commonly causes sores on the lips (known as fever blisters or cold sores), but it can cause genital infections as well. HSV type 2 most often causes genital sores, but it also can infect the mouth.

Both HSV 1 and 2 can produce sores in and around the vaginal area, on the penis, around the anal opening, and on the buttocks or thighs. Occasionally, sores also appear on other parts of the body where broken skin has come into contact with HSV. The virus remains in certain nerve cells of the body for life, causing periodic symptoms in some people.

Genital herpes infection usually is acquired by sexual contact with someone who unknowingly is having an asymptomatic outbreak of herpes sores in the genital area. People with oral herpes can transmit the infection to the genital area of a partner during oral-genital sex. Herpes infections also can be transmitted by a person who is infected with HSV who has noticeable symptoms. The virus is spread only rarely, if at all, by contact with objects such as a toilet seat or hot tub.

GENITAL WARTS/HPV

Human papilloma virus (HPV) is one of the most common causes of sexually transmitted disease (STD) in the world. Experts estimate that as many as 24 million Americans are infected with HPV, and the frequency of infection and disease appears to be increasing.

More than 60 types of HPV have been identified by scientists. Some types of the virus cause common skin warts. About one-third of the HPV types is spread through sexual contact and lives only in genital tissue. Low-risk types of HPV cause genital warts, the most recognizable sign of genital HPV infection. Other high-risk types of HPV cause cervical cancer and other genital cancers.

Like many sexually transmitted organisms, HPV usually causes a silent infection— that is, one that does not have visible symptoms. One study sponsored by the National Institute of Allergy and Infectious Diseases (NIAID) reported that almost half of the women infected with HPV had no obvious symptoms. Because the viral infection persists, individuals may not be aware of their infection or the potential risk of transmission to others and of developing complications.

GONORRHEA

Approximately 400,000 cases of gonorrhea are reported to the CDC each year in this country. Gonorrhea is caused by Neisseria Gonorrhoeae. The most common symptoms of infection are a discharge from the vagina or penis and painful or difficult urination. The most common and serious complications occur in women and, as with chlamydial infection, these complications include PID, ectopic pregnancy, and infertility.

Historically, penicillin has been used to treat gonorrhea, but in the last decade, four types of antibiotic resistance have emerged. New antibiotics or combinations of drugs must be used to treat these resistant strains.

SYPHILIS

The incidence of syphilis has increased and decreased dramatically in recent years, with more than 11,000 cases reported in 1996. Syphilis is caused by Treponema Pallidum. The first symptoms of infection may go undetected because they are very mild and disappear spontaneously. The initial symptom is a chancre; it is usually a painless open sore that usually appears on the penis or around or in the vagina. It can also occur near the mouth, anus, or on the hands. If untreated, syphilis may go on to more advanced stages, including a transient rash and, eventually, serious involvement of the heart and central nervous system. The full course of the disease can take years. Penicillin remains the most effective drug to treat people with syphilis.

VIRAL HEPATITIS

Hepatitis A is a cause of acute hepatitis. Fewer than 5 percent of infections are transmitted through fecal-oral contact during sexual intercourse, mostly among men who have sex with men (MSM).

Hepatitis B virus (HBV) infection is an STD with severe complications including chronic hepatitis, cirrhosis, and liver carcinoma. Of approximately 200,000 new HBV infections in the U.S. each year, approximately half are transmitted through sexual intercourse. Preliminary data from a large U.S. multisite study indicate that approximately one third of persons with acute hepatitis B virus infections in 1995 had a history of another STD. In addition to hepatitis B, several other types of viral hepatitis can be transmitted sexually.

Hepatitis C virus, the most common cause of non-A and non-B hepatitis, causes chronic liver disease in most infected adults. The efficiency of sexual and perinatal transmission of this virus, however, is much less than that for HBV or HIV.

Hepatitis D (delta) virus is a virus that can be sexually transmitted but requires the presence of hepatitis B virus to replicate. Although hepatitis D virus can be transmitted sexually, it is less efficiently transmitted through sexual intercourse compared to HBV.

At present, there are no specific treatments for the acute symptoms of viral hepatitis. Doctors recommend bedrest, a healthy diet, and avoidance of alcoholic beverages. A genetically engineered form of a naturally occurring protein, interferon alpha, is used to treat people with chronic hepatitis C. Studies supported by the National Institute of Health led to the approval of interferon alpha for the treatment of those with chronic HBV as well.

OTHER STDS

Other diseases that may be sexually transmitted include trichomoniasis, bacterial vaginosis, cytomegalovirus infections, scabies, and pubic lice. For information on these diseases and others, visit the STD section of the National Institute of Allergy and Infectious Diseases (NIAID) Web site.

WHO IS BEING INFECTED?

In the United States alone, an estimated 15.3 million new cases of STDs are reported each year. This table shows the incidence and prevalence of some of the most common STDs.

STD1	*Incidence	**Prevalence
Chlamydia	3,000,000	2,000,000
Gonorrhea	650,000	***
Syphilis	70,000	***
Herpes (HSV)	1,000,000	45,000,000
Hepatitis B (HBV)	120,000	417,000
Genital Warts / Human Papilloma Virus (HPV)	5,500,000	20,000,000
Trichomoniasis	5,000,000	***

* Estimated number of new cases each year
** Estimated number of people currently infected
*** No recent surveys on national prevalence for gonorrhea, syphilis, or trichomoniasis have been conducted.

VARIATIONS IN RISK

STDs affect men and women of all backgrounds and economic levels. However, STDs disproportionately affect women, infants, young people, and minorities. STDs are most prevalent among teens and young adults with nearly two-thirds of all STDs occurring in people under age 25.

Some contributing factors in the rise of STDs include the facts that young people have become sexually active earlier, divorce is more common, and sexually active people are more likely to have multiple sex partners.

WHAT ARE SOME HEALTH RISKS OF STD INFECTION?

STDs can result in irreparable lifetime damage, including blindness, bone deformities, mental retardation, and death for infants infected by their mothers during gestation or birth.

In women, STDs can lead to pelvic inflammatory disease (PID), infertility, potentially fatal ectopic pregnancies, and cancer of the reproductive tract.

The most reliable ways to avoid becoming infected with or transmitting STDs are:

- Abstain from sexual intercourse (i.e., oral, vaginal, or anal sex)
- Be in a long-term, mutually monogamous relationship with an uninfected partner

REDUCING YOUR RISK OF STD INFECTION

All partners should get tested for HIV and other STDs before initiating sexual intercourse. However, if you decide to be sexually active with a partner whose infection status is unknown or who is infected with HIV or another STD, you can reduce your risk of contracting an STD:

- Ask a new sex partner if he or she has an STD, has been exposed to one, or has any unexplained physical symptoms. Do not have sex if your partner has signs or symptoms of STDs, such as sores, rashes, or discharge from the genital area. Many common STDs have no symptoms but can still be transmitted to a sexual partner. If your partner has had sexual relations with someone else recently, he or she may have an STD, even if there are no symptoms.
- Use a new condom for each act of insertive intercourse.
- Get regular checkups for STDs (even if you show no symptoms), and become familiar with the common symptoms. Most STDs are readily treated, and the earlier treatment is sought and sex partners are warned, the less likely the disease will do irreparable damage.

Cancer

Cancer is caused when a cell's DNA is damaged, causing it to reproduce unnecessarily. A group of these extra cells is called a tumor. Some tumors, called cancerous or malignant, spread through the body, which makes them more dangerous. In addition to being able to spread, malignant tumors also grow relatively quickly. The cancerous cells spread by attacking cells in nearby tissue and organs. Breast, liver and colon cancer are all examples of cancers with malignant tumors. On the other hand, a benign tumor does not spread, and grows relatively slowly. They can be found in various places in the body. These tumors can still be dangerous, but they remain localized, and once removed don't generally grow back. A mole is an example of a benign tumor.

There are four classifications of cancer:

1. Carcinomas – tissue covering body surfaces and lining of body cavities, mouth, breast
2. Sarcomas – bones, muscles and connective tissue
3. Lymphomas – in the infection-fighting regions

4. Leukemia – cancer of the blood-forming regions, including bone marrow and spleen

Malignant neoplasms are the leading cause of death in women ages 35-64, while for men it is cardiovascular disease. A malignant neoplasm is the scientific way of stating cancer, including 100 subtypes of cancer. Neoplasm refers to the explosive overgrowth of new cells, sticking together to create tumors.

The list of common cancers includes cancers that are diagnosed with the greatest frequency in the United States. Cancer incidence statistics from the American Cancer Society and other resources were used to create the list. To qualify as a common cancer, the estimated annual incidence for 2005 had to be 25,000 cases or more.

- Bladder Cancer
- Breast Cancer
- Colon and Rectal Cancer
- Endometrial Cancer
- Kidney Cancer (Renal Cell)
- Leukemia
- Thyroid Cancer
- Lung Cancer
- Melanoma
- Non-Hodgkin's Lymphoma
- Pancreatic Cancer
- Prostate Cancer
- Skin (Non-melanoma)

The most common type of cancer on the list is non-melanoma skin cancer, with more than 1,000,000 new cases expected in the United States in 2005. Non-melanoma skin cancers represent about half of all cancers diagnosed in this country.

The cancers on the list with the lowest incidence are renal cell cancer of the kidney and thyroid cancer. The estimated number of new cases of kidney cancer (renal cell and renal pelvis) for 2005 is 36,160. Approximately 70% of all kidney cancers are renal cell cancers, suggesting that slightly more than 25,000 new cases of renal cell cancer will be diagnosed in 2005. The estimated number of new cases of thyroid cancer for 2005 is 25,690.

Because colon and rectal cancers are often referred to as "colorectal cancers", these two cancer types were combined for the list. For 2005, the estimated number of new cases of colon cancer is 104,950, and the estimated number of new cases of rectal cancer is 40,340. These numbers are slightly smaller than those estimated for 2004.

Leukemia as a cancer type includes acute lymphoblastic (or lymphoid) leukemia, chronic lymphocytic leukemia, acute myeloid leukemia, chronic myelogenous (or myeloid) leukemia, and other forms of leukemia. It is estimated that more than 34,000 new cases of leukemia will be diagnosed in the United States in 2005, with acute myeloid leukemia being the most common type (approximately 12,000 new cases). The total number of new leukemia cases estimated for 2005 is slightly larger than the number estimated for 2004.

Lung Cancer

Tobacco smoking causes 90% of all lung cancers. Contributing factors are smoking cigars or pipes, and second-hand smoke. Exposure to many gases at work or in the environment are also thought to increase risks. Possible risk factors are air pollution and insufficient consumption of fruits.

Skin Cancer

Skin cancer (melanoma) affects both men and women. Any change in size or color of moles should be checked by a skin cancer specialist. Risk factors include excessive exposure to sun, fair skin, personal or family history of melanoma, and reduced renal function due to organ transplants. Melanoma occurs almost exclusively in whites.

Breast Cancer

Risk factors are family history (especially mother or sister) and a personal history of breast, ovarian, or endometrial cancer. Possible risk factors are dietary fat and physical inactivity. Breast cancer also occurs in men. For men, risk factors include increasing age, family history, radiation exposure, and having high levels of estrogen.

Prostate Cancer

Risk factors include prostatic hyperplasia (enlarged prostate), a family history, especially a father or brother. Possible risk factors are diets high in animal fats, hormonal factors, smoking, alcohol, and physical inactivity. Black males have much higher rates of prostate cancers than white males.

Ovary

Risk factors are personal history of breast cancer, a family history of breast or ovarian cancer, and never bearing children. The risk may be reduced by tubal ligation or hysterectomy.

Hodgkin Disease

Risk factors are infectious mononucleosis and Epstein-Barr virus infection. A possible risk factor is a family history of Hodgkin lymphoma.

Brain

Risk factors are largely genetic factors, being a parent or child with brain cancer. Possible risk factors are exposure to electromagnetic fields, exposure to farm animals and pets, severe head trauma, and loud noise.

Thyroid

Risk factors are high doses of ionizing radiation and goiter.

Since the types and risk factors of cancer are so many, the best preventative step you can take is having regular physical examinations by your family doctor. In addition, women should begin self-examination of breasts at about age 20. Mammograms should begin about age 40 and continue for life. It is imperative that women have annual Pap smears.

If possible, go to the same doctor or imaging center for your Pap smears and mammograms. It is important that you build up a medical history in these areas. Particularly, if you change imaging centers for your mammogram, that lab must set a new base line for the results.

Both men and women should have periodic (as recommended by your doctor) colonoscopies. Men should have annual screenings for prostate cancer. This process may include a rectal exam, along with a PSA (prostate-specific antigens) blood test. Skin cancer affects both men and women. Any change in size or color of moles should be checked by a skin cancer specialist.

PREVENTION

Although we don't know what causes cancer, we know that there are several things that can be done to reduce one's chances significantly:

- Don't smoke or use tobacco
- Proper exercise
- Proper diet
- Use sunblock (to prevent melanoma)
- Proper screenings for your gender and age group

There are several cancer warning signs including:

- Changes in bladder and bowel habits
- Unusual bleeding
- A sore that doesn't heal
- Lump in breast or elsewhere on the body

- Difficulty swallowing or indigestion
- Change in wart or mole
- Nagging cough or hoarseness

Cancer-related checkups should be done every three years for people 20-40 and every year for 40 and older. Women should have an annual mammogram and know how to check themselves each month for lumps.

TREATMENT

Radiotherapy uses radiation to kill cancerous cells while chemotherapy uses drugs to kill cancerous cells. Immunotherapy is a new technique that uses the body's own disease fighting system.

Cardiovascular Disease

More people die from cardiovascular disease than from any other cause, except for teenagers, for whom the leading cause of death is accidents. Cardiovascular diseases (CVDs) are diseases of the heart and blood vessels. The cardiovascular system consists of the heart and blood vessels that transport nutrients, oxygen, hormones, etc., throughout the body and regulates temperature, the water levels of cells and acidity levels.

The heart is the body's largest muscle, a four-chambered pump, roughly the size of a man's fist. The top two chambers are called the atria which receive blood. Ventricles are the lower chambers of the heart which pump blood through the blood vessels. Arteries are what carry the blood away from the heart to the rest of the body. Capillaries are the small blood vessels that branch out from the arterioles, which are branches of the arteries. When the arteries harden and thicken, it is called atherosclerosis. Arteriosclerosis is when there are deposits of fatty substances and other waste products that line the artery. Plaque makes up the deposits in the arteries.

Of all the major types of cardiovascular disease, coronary heart disease is the single greatest killer. A heart attack is a blockage of blood supply to the heart. Another name for heart attack is a myocardial infarction. This happens when there is a blood clot (coronary thrombosis) blocking an artery. Ischemia is reduced oxygen supply to the heart. To clear blockage, an angioplasty can be administered, which is when a catheter with a balloon tip is inserted into the artery and the balloon is inflated to clear the blockage. Angina pectoris is severe chest pain occurring as a result of reduced oxygen flow to the heart. Stroke happens when the brain is damaged by disrupted blood supply. Arrhythmia is an irregularity in heartbeat. Fibrillation is a sporadic heartbeat, resulting in inefficiency in moving blood through the cardiovascular system. An aneurysm is a weakened blood vessel that may bulge or burst under pressure.

Heart failure doesn't actually mean that the heart suddenly stops working altogether. In the case of congestive heart failure, the problem is that the heart isn't circulating enough blood through the body. This could be because the heart itself is weak, or it could be the result of other types of heart disease. When blood flow to the kidney decreases, it filters less fluid out of the blood stream and that fluid begins to build up in other places such as the lungs, liver, and around the eyes. It some cases it can even cause the ankles and legs to swell. This buildup of fluid causes a number of other symptoms. Fatigue is a general symptom of congestive heart failure. Fluid in the lungs causes shortness of breath, and in some cases the person can't sleep unless they are sitting upright. Fluid in the liver and intestines causes nausea.

Hypertension is sustained elevated blood pressure. Systolic pressure measures the pressure on the walls of the arteries when the heart contracts, versus its opposite, diastolic pressure, which indicates the pressure when the heart is at the relaxation phase.

Cardiomyopathy is the term for any problem or disease which causes decreased function of the heart. There are two basic types of cardiomyopathy. The first is hypertrophic cardiomyopathy, which is when the tissue in the heart hardens. The second is congestive cardiomyopathy, which is when the heart weakens and fails.

The most common cause of heart disease is the narrowing or blockage of the coronary arteries. This is commonly referred to as CHD (Coronary Heart Disease) or CAD. CAD (Coronary Artery Disease) is the most common type of heart disease. CAD results when the arteries carrying blood to the heart become narrow or hardened. This condition is caused by a buildup of cholesterol and other materials (plaque) on the inner walls of the arteries. Consequently, less blood flows through the arteries. As a result, the heart muscle cannot get enough blood or oxygen, each of which is vital to its functioning.

Since CAD may also weaken the heart muscle, it may contribute to heart failure and arrhythmias (irregular heartbeats). This may lead to chest pain (angina) or a heart attack.

The heart is designed so that blood only flows in one direction. The mitral valve separates the upper and lower sections of the left side of the heart. When the mitral valve doesn't close properly it is called mitral valve prolapse or MVP. If the mitral valve isn't closing properly, it can allow blood to flow "backwards" when the heart contracts. This can cause an increased risk of infections, and other health problems.

To help you understand the importance of understanding heart disease, the following facts may amaze you:

- Coronary artery disease causes 1.2 million heart attacks a year, and over 40 percent of those will die.
- More seriously, 350,000 people with heart attacks will die in the emergency room or before they reach the hospital.
- According to the American Heart Association, more than 7 million people have suffered a heart attack in their lifetimes.

If we are to reduce those statistics, it is imperative that all of us understand the risk factors for heart disease and take steps to eliminate them. Risk factors for heart disease are of two types: controllable and uncontrollable.

CARDIOVASCULAR DISEASE RISK FACTORS

Uncontrollable Risk Factors:

- **Gender:** More men than women develop heart disease, but that fact is changing. The number of females who develop heart disease is rising.
- **Race:** Hispanics, African-Americans and American Indians have a higher rate of heart disease than Caucasians.
- **Increasing Age:** It has been reported that 83 percent of people who die of coronary heart disease are 65 or older. The risk increases for men 55 years and older; for women, 65 years and older.

Controllable Risk Factors:

- **Smoking:** The use of tobacco has been proven inconclusively to contribute to heart disease. Cigarette smoking carries the highest risk, cigar and pipe smokers are also at a higher risk than non-smokers. Second-hand smoke is also a contributing factor.
- **Overweight:** People who are overweight, particularly if much of the body weight is at the waistline, are at a higher risk of heart disease.
- **High Blood Pressure (HBP):** High blood pressure, also known as hypertension, is a major risk factor for heart disease. A blood pressure reading is expressed in two numbers. A blood pressure number of 140 over 90 represents a major risk. The upper number (140) is the systolic number. The lower number (90) is the diastolic number. Ask your doctor what your BP should be. It is startling to realize that 80 million Americans have high blood pressure.
- **Physical Activity:** An inactive (sedentary) life style increases your risk of developing cardiovascular disease.
- **Diabetes mellitus:** Diabetes seriously increases your risk of developing cardiovascular disease. Even when your blood sugar is controlled, you are at risk. The risk is even greater if your blood sugar is not controlled.

- **Stress:** Researchers are divided on whether stress in itself is a risk factor for heart disease, but they are in agreement that the individual's response to stress can be a contributing factor. People who feel stressed may eat or smoke too much, thus triggering other risk factors. In some severely stressed people, their blood pressure may rise significantly, thus triggering another factor.

CARDIOVASCULAR HEALTH PREVENTION

How can you prevent cardiovascular problems?

- **Quit Smoking.** You would have to be living in a vacuum not to be aware of the dangers of smoking. If you are a smoker, quit now! No more excuses, no more promises to do it later, do it today! By continuing to smoke, you are not only increasing your own risks, your second-hand smoke is putting those around you at risk. If you are a young person, it is not "cool" to smoke. It's foolish! You would be hard pressed to find an adult smoker who does not regret ever starting.
- **Lose weight.** If you are overweight, a good place to start is at your doctor's office. Your doctor is able to measure your BMI (Body Mass Index) as a guide to how much weight you should lose and even help you develop a nutritional plan to help you achieve a healthy weight. Losing weight is never fun. You may not lose as quickly as you would like; but it helps to remember, you didn't put the weight on overnight and it's not going to disappear in a day or two. Avoid crash diets. It's hard on your body to "balloon" and then reduce repeatedly. Dieting should be a change in life style; eat healthy at every meal.
- **Exercise.** It is important to stay physically active. You are never too young or too old to exercise. Research shows that physical activity can reduce the risk of heart disease. The type of exercise you do will, of course be determined by your physical condition and age. Physical activity that is of the right frequency, intensity, and duration does wonders for your body. Injury frequently occurs in those who have been physically inactive for a long time. Injury can be avoided by taking a gradual, but regular, approach to exercise.
- **Diet.** Avoid foods fried in saturated fat. Reducing your fat intake will not only lower your cholesterol but also help to lower your blood pressure. Olive, canola and other plant based oils are good choices for unsaturated fats. If you maintain a healthy weight, restrict sodium intake and dietary fats, and your blood pressure is still too high, your doctor will probably recommend that you begin a regimen of blood pressure medication. Before starting on this medication, be sure to ask your doctor to explain its benefits thoroughly and also to alert you to any possible side effects.
- **Limit Alcohol.** Drink alcohol in moderation. The recommended daily levels are two drinks per day for men; women, one drink per day. "Drink size" is measured as 12 ounces of beer, a 5-oz. glass of wine.

- **Stress.** Avoid stressful situations as much as possible. A good bit of advice is to never become stressed over a situation or problem you cannot change. Much of the stress we feel is self-imposed. Very few situations or problems we encounter are worth getting stressed out about.

PREVENTATIVE SCREENINGS

Medical personnel are now advising their patients to have the following screening tests for heart disease:

MEN	WOMEN
Cholesterol	Mammogram
Blood pressure	Pap smear
Colorectal cancer	Cholesterol
Prostate cancer	Blood pressure
Colorectal cancer	
Osteoporosis	

After you have had an initial screening in these areas, your doctor will advise you when to have repeat screenings.

Blood Pressure

Blood pressure is the amount of pressure in the blood veins. It is expressed in two numbers, the first of which represents the systolic pressure. The systolic pressure is the amount of pressure during a heartbeat when the heart contracts. The second number is the diastolic pressure, and is the pressure when the heart is relaxed between beats. The two numbers are expressed as a fraction. For example, if a person's systolic pressure was 130, and their diastolic pressure was 85, it would be written 130/85, and pronounced "130 over 85."

Blood pressure is classified in four basic groups. Normal blood pressure is considered to be below 120 systolic and below 80 diastolic. Blood pressure between 120-139 systolic and 80-89 diastolic is considered to be pre-hypertensive. Neither of these two stages are considered urgent or dangerous. Hypertension is a continuous state of high blood pressure, and is sometimes called the "silent killer" because it doesn't have any symptoms. Anything above 140/90 is considered hypertensive. There are two levels of hypertension. The first, stage 1 hypertension, is considered to be anything from 140-159 systolic and 90-99 diastolic. Stage 2 hypertension is considered to be anything above 160 systolic and 100 diastolic. If the two pressures are in different ranges, the higher number is used.

Stroke

Strokes are the third leading cause of death, following heart disease and cancer. Coronary diseases and strokes are closely related. In fact, they are so closely related that the American Stroke Association (ASA) is a division of the American Heart Association (AHA).

Let's begin with a definition of a stroke. A stroke is the rapid loss of brain function when the blood supply to some or all parts of the brain.

Strokes are usually one of three types: ischemic, hemorrhagic, and thrombotic. Ischemic strokes strike quickly and last only a few minutes or a few hours. The person may or may not have any residual weaknesses. Ischemic strokes are usually referred to as TIAs (transient ischemic activity). A TIA strikes quickly, usually without warning. A TIA is a warning that a stroke may occur soon. Thrombotic strokes are characterized as ischemic. In fact, 80 percent of all strokes are ischemic. This slows the flow of oxygen and nutrients to the brain. Hemorrhagic strokes are much more serious, and some residual damage almost always results.

The most common is ischemic stroke. Ischemic strokes account for over 80% of all strokes. These types of strokes happen when there is a clot or other type of blockage in an artery leading to the brain. When the blood flow to the brain is stopped, the brain cells can't function properly. If the blockage lasts more than a few minutes it can cause permanent damage, or death.

What are the symptoms of a stroke? Symptoms do appear, but they are often ignored. Advocates of stroke prevention and treatment have defined a 3-step procedure that should be followed if you suspect someone is having a stroke:

(1) Ask the person to smile. Does one side of the face droop?
(2) Ask the person to raise both arms. Does one arm drift downward?
(3) Ask the person to repeat a simple sentence. Are the words slurred? Can he/she repeat the sentence correctly?

If the person has any of these symptoms, time is critical. Brain cells are dying. Call 9-1-1 or get to the hospital fast.

What preventative steps can be taken to lower the risk of having a stroke? The risk factors and preventative measures for stroke are the same as those given for heart disease. Refer back to the discussion of coronary risk factors.

Unfortunately, if you have several of the risk factors, it does not always mean you will have a stroke. Likewise, if you have none of the risk factors, it does not always mean that you will not have a stroke.

Chronic Disorders

By definition, the term chronic means long, drawn out, or of long duration. In use, the term chronic generally describes a condition for which there is a treatment but no cure.

Categories of chronic diseases include the following body areas:

- Pulmonary disorder
- Musculoskeletal
- Skin
- Motor tic
- Stomach
- Vocal tic
- Pain

Pulmonary Disorders

Pulmonary disorders (commonly known as COPD—Chronic Obstructive Pulmonary Disease) affect 16 million people. Examples are chronic bronchitis, emphysema, and asthma. Thus, emphysema is a persistent disease affecting the rate of airflow through the lungs. The primary risk factor for emphysema is cigarette smoking. There is some thought that emphysema is hereditary, but this has not been conclusively proven; studies of this possibility continue. Working in an environment polluted by chemical fumes or dust definitely increases the risk of developing emphysema.

Chronic musculoskeletal disease refers to the skeleton, particularly to those muscles which are attached to the skeleton. Some of the diseases covered by this classification are arthritis, rheumatism, and fibromyalgia.

Fibromyalgia

About 3.7 million Americans suffer from fibromyalgia. Fibromyalgia is the second most common rheumatic condition. It differs from true arthritis in that it affects the ligaments and muscles of the body rather than the joints. Patients have pain, aching, and general stiffness all over the body. Fibromyalgia often worsens under the following conditions:

- Psychological stress
- Physical exertion
- Cold weather
- Change in barometric pressure
- Lack of deep sleep

Fibromyalgia strikes females more than male. It typically strikes between the ages of 20 and 60. There is no cure for fibromyalgia, but the right treatment can greatly alleviate the aches and pains.

Eczema

Eczema reveals itself as an itchy, scaling, swelling skin rash. Eczema is caused by an allergic reaction. It also tends to appear in people suffering from hay fever and asthma. Of course, the obvious advice is to avoid the product causing the reaction. However, isolating a single allergen can be a tricky process. Some of the common allergens (any substance that brings on manifestations of an allergy) are household cleaners, after-shave lotions, soaps, and perfumed products. If your eczema is a serious problem, you may want to see a dermatologist (a doctor who specializes in diseases of the skin).

Rosacea

Rosacea is another type of chronic skin disorder. It may start as a blush across your nose and face. It then evolves into a rash. Rosacea is a common disorder, affecting an estimated 14 million Americans. Unfortunately, only a small fraction of infected persons seek help. If you exhibit any of the following signs, see a doctor for diagnosis and treatment.

- Redness on cheeks, nose, chin, or forehead
- Small, visible blood vessels on the face
- Bumps or pimples on the face
- Watery or irritated eyes

Like eczema, the cause of rosacea is unknown, but medical treatment for it is available.

Chronic Stomach Disorders

Stomach disorders are common to many people. We all know the misery a bout of flu causes us. We experience nausea, vomiting, perhaps diarrhea, and a general feeling of malaise. We feel so relieved when the "bug" has worked its way out of us, and we begin to feel healthy again. It may be hard to believe but many, many people know stomach distress as a daily feeling. What are the causes of this chronic condition, and what can we do to restore our healthy stomach?

There are many common chronic stomach diseases we could explore. They include gastritis, gastroenteritis, Crohn's disease, hepatitis, hernia, appendicitis, and peptic ulcer. For this study we will explore probably the most common form of chronic stomach diseases: gastroenteritis. That's a big word, so let's break it down. Gastro refers to the stomach; enteritis means inflammation. Thus, gastroenteritis is an inflammation of the stomach.

First, let's look at the anatomical description of the disease. We need to learn two additional medical terms to fully understand gastroenteritis. Those words are pancreas and duodenum. The pancreas is a long, irregularly shaped gland lying behind the stomach that plays a critical role in digestion. The duodenum is the beginning of the small intestine. The pancreas secretes digestive enzymes into the duodenum.

So what is gastroenteritis? Gastroenteritis is the functioning of pancreatic juices in the duodenum before reaching the stomach. When this happens, bacteria form in the stomach lining and become inflamed. Diarrhea, abdominal cramp, nausea, and loss of appetite may occur.

The treatment for gastroenteritis includes no smoking and no alcohol consumption.

If the diarrhea is severe, give the patient an abundance of liquids to avoid the onset of dehydration. The most important part of the treatment is to replace the fluids the patient lost through vomiting and diarrhea.

Autoimmune Disease

Just what is an autoimmune disease? To understand autoimmune diseases, we need to review the role our immune system plays in our body. The role of the immune system is to protect the body against attacks by germs and other foreign objects. The immune system must learn this operation over time. Autoimmune problems arise when the immune system fails to distinguish between healthy and unhealthy immunes. To put it even more simply, think of the healthy immunes as being the "good guys," the ones wearing the "white hats" in old-time Westerns. The unhealthy antibodies are the "bad guys," the ones in the black hats. An autoimmune problem develops when our antibodies cannot distinguish between the good guys and the bad guys. As a result, they attack and destroy the good guys. The bad guys take control of our bodies and diseases result.

It is not known why this occurs in some people and not in others. It is thought that a combination of genetic, environmental, and hormonal elements are involved.

A few of the better known autoimmune diseases are:

- Crohn's disease
- Diabetes
- Fibromyalgia
- Lupus
- Multiple sclerosis
- Sjogren's disease
- Rheumatoid arthritis

Multiple Sclerosis

The Epstein-Barr virus, or EBV is one of the most common viruses. If contracted while a person is in their teens or younger, the symptoms aren't very noticeable. However, if it is contracted after teenage years it is likely to cause infectious mononucleosis. It is thought that the Epstein-Barr virus might be a possible cause of multiple sclerosis because people who have multiple sclerosis have higher than expected amounts of antibodies for the EBV.

Multiple sclerosis or MS is a disease in which a person's immune system begins to attack their nervous system. In some cases, the symptoms come on quickly, but usually it is a gradual process. MS is also characterized by periods of remission between periods of worsening. It is treated with medicines which attempt to slow the progression and reduce symptoms.

Sjogren's Disease

Sjogren's disease is a lesser known autoimmune disease, but it affects 2 million Americans. Women represent 90% of the victims of this disease. The exact cause of Sjogren's disease is not known, but it is increasingly believed to be a genetic disorder. It is more commonly found in families where other family members have developed an autoimmune disease.

Sjogren's is demonstrated by an inflammation of the glands, particularly those that produce fluid. The major areas are the mouth and the eyes. Extreme dryness exists in these areas. Sjogren's is sometimes considered systemic since it can affect other organs of the body. There is no cure for Sjogren's, but the disease typically strikes between the ages of 20 and 60.

Sickle Cell Disease

Sickle cell disease, or sickle cell anemia, is a genetic disease in which a person has an abnormal type of hemoglobin. Hemoglobin is an oxygen carrying protein which gives red blood cells their color. When a person has the abnormal hemoglobin, called sickle hemoglobin, it causes crystals to form in the cells which give it a twisted and rigid shape. This can cause problems with blood flow, which can result in organ damage.

This disease is most common among African Americans.

Rheumatoid Arthritis

Two million Americans suffer from rheumatoid arthritis, the cause of which is unknown. Some hopeful research is being done in Japan, where a potentially helpful protein has been isolated.

Rheumatoid arthritis is a common rheumatic condition. It differs from true arthritis in that it affects the ligaments and muscles of the body rather than the joints. Patients have pain, aching, and general stiffness all over the body.

Diabetes

Diabetes is a disease that is caused when the pancreas does not produce enough insulin, or the body doesn't respond to it normally. Insulin is a hormone that transfers glucose from the blood stream, into the liver, muscle, and fat cells. Glucose is used by those cells for fuel, so when the insulin isn't present the cells don't have that fuel source. Some of the symptoms of diabetes include: fatigue, weight gain, blurry vision, frequent urination, excessive thirst, and hunger. The exact cause of diabetes isn't known, however, there are factors which cause increased risk of developing type II diabetes. They include being over 45, being overweight, being related to a person with diabetes, and having high blood pressure.

There are two types of diabetes. Type I diabetes can also be called juvenile onset diabetes, because it generally manifests earlier in life. Usually a person with type I diabetes is diagnosed by the time they are 14. Type I diabetes is when a person's immune system destroys the cells which make insulin. This means the person is insulin-dependent, and for the rest of their lives must have insulin injections or take medication orally.

Type II diabetes generally develops gradually, and later in life. Usually, people with type II diabetes are diagnosed when they are middle age or later. It is also called adult-onset diabetes because of this, however there has been an increased occurrence of diagnosis in younger people due to poor health habits. Type II diabetes is when a person's liver, muscle and fat cells don't respond normally to insulin, and because of this the glucose in the blood stream can't be stored in the cells as energy. People with type II diabetes can often control their symptoms by maintaining proper weight and exercise routines.

A third type of diabetes called gestational diabetes can develop in a woman during pregnancy. The condition generally disappears after she gives birth.

Arthritis

Arthritis strikes one in seven Americans. Arthritis is a painful inflammatory disease of the joints which results in loss of ability to use the hands, especially in tasks where precision is necessary such as sewing, embroidering, etc. Osteoarthritis is a progressive deterioration of the bones and joints which is associated with the Wear and Tear Theory of Aging. It is the most common form of osteoarthritis. This type of arthritis is associated with the Wear and Tear Theory of Aging because it is a gradual deterioration of bones and joints. Age, previous injuries, abnormal use, and heredity are all causes of osteoarthritis.

Albinism

From the National Organization of Albinism and Hyperpigmentation, the following is information about the disease: "People with albinism have little or no pigment in their eyes, skin, or hair. They have inherited genes that do not make the usual amounts of a pigment called melanin. When both parents carry the gene, and neither parent has albinism, there is a one in four chance at each pregnancy that the baby will be born with albinism. This type of inheritance is called autosomal recessive inheritance. People who have it are sometimes called Albinos. Albinism can affect people from all races."

Tay-Sachs Disease

The National Institute of Neurological Disorders and Strokes published the following information on Tay-Sachs disease:

WHAT IS TAY-SACHS DISEASE?

Tay-Sachs disease is a fatal genetic disorder in which harmful quantities of a fatty substance called ganglioside GM2 accumulate in the nerve cells in the brain. Infants with Tay-Sachs disease appear to develop normally for the first few months of life. Then, as nerve cells become distended with fatty material, a relentless deterioration of mental and physical abilities occurs. The child becomes blind, deaf, and unable to swallow. Muscles begin to atrophy and paralysis sets in. A much rarer form of the disorder which occurs in patients in their twenties and early thirties is characterized by unsteadiness of gait and progressive neurological deterioration. Patients with Tay-Sachs have a "cherry-red" spot in the back of their eyes. The condition is caused by insufficient activity of an enzyme called hexosaminidase A that catalyzes the biodegradation of acidic fatty materials known as gangliosides. Gangliosides are made and biodegraded rapidly in early life as the brain develops. Patients and carriers of Tay-Sachs disease can be identified by a simple blood test that measures hexosaminidase A activity. Both parents must be carriers in order to have an affected child. When both parents are found to carry a genetic mutation in hexosaminidase A, there is a 25 percent chance with each pregnancy that the child will be affected with Tay-Sachs disease. Prenatal monitoring of pregnancies is available if desired.

IS THERE ANY TREATMENT?

Presently there is no treatment for Tay-Sachs.

WHAT IS THE PROGNOSIS?

Even with the best of care, children with Tay-Sachs disease usually die by age 5.

Cystic Fibrosis

Cystic fibrosis (CF) is a chronic, progressive, and frequently fatal genetic (inherited) disease of the body's mucus glands. CF primarily affects the respiratory and digestive systems in children and young adults. The sweat glands and the reproductive system are also usually involved. On the average, individuals with CF have a lifespan of approximately 30 years. CF-like disease has been known for over two centuries. The name, cystic fibrosis of the pancreas, was first applied to the disease in 1938.

According to the data collected by the Cystic Fibrosis Foundation, there are about 30,000 Americans, 3,000 Canadians, and 20,000 Europeans with CF. The disease occurs mostly in whites whose ancestors came from northern Europe, although it affects all races and ethnic groups. Accordingly, it is less common in African Americans, Native Americans, and Asian Americans. Approximately 2,500 babies are born with CF each year in the United States. Also, about 1 in every 20 Americans is an unaffected carrier of an abnormal "CF gene." These 12 million people are usually unaware that they are carriers.

CF does not follow the same pattern in all patients but affects different people in different ways and to varying degrees. However, the basic problem is the same-an abnormality in the glands, which produce or secrete sweat and mucus. Sweat cools the body; mucus lubricates the respiratory, digestive, and reproductive systems, and prevents tissues from drying out, protecting them from infection.

People with CF lose excessive amounts of salt when they sweat. This can upset the balance of minerals in the blood, which may cause abnormal heart rhythms. Going into shock is also a risk.

Mucus in CF patients is very thick and accumulates in the intestines and lungs. The result is malnutrition, poor growth, frequent respiratory infections, breathing difficulties, and eventually permanent lung damage. Lung disease is the usual cause of death in most patients.

CF can cause various other medical problems. These include sinusitis (inflammation of the nasal sinuses, which are cavities in the skull behind, above, and on both sides of the nose), nasal polyps (fleshy growths inside the nose), clubbing (rounding and enlargement of fingers and toes), pneumothorax (rupture of lung tissue and trapping of air between the lung and the chest wall), hemoptysis (coughing of blood), corpulmonale (enlargement of the right side of the heart), abdominal pain and discomfort, gassiness (too much gas in the intestine), and rectal prolapse (protrusion of the rectum through the anus). Liver disease, diabetes, inflammation of the pancreas, and gallstones also occur in some people with CF.

Genes are the basic units of heredity. They are located on structures within the cell nucleus called chromosomes. The function of most genes is to instruct the cells to make particular proteins, most of which have important life-sustaining roles.

Every human being has 46 chromosomes, 23 inherited from each parent. Because each of the 23 pairs of chromosomes contains a complete set of genes, every individual has two sets (one from each parent) of genes for each function. In some individuals, the basic building blocks of a gene (called base pairs) are altered (mutated). A mutation can cause the body to make a defective protein or no protein at all. The result is a loss of some essential biological function and that leads to disease.

Children may inherit altered genes from one or both parents.

Diseases such as CF that are caused by inherited genes are called genetic diseases. In CF, each parent carries one abnormal CF gene and one normal CF gene but shows no evidence of the disease because the normal CF gene dominates or "recesses" the abnormal CF gene. To have CF, a child must inherit two abnormal genes-one from each parent. The recessive CF gene can occur in both boys and girls because it is located on non-sex-linked chromosomes called autosomal chromosomes. CF is therefore called an autosomal recessive genetic disease.

The inheritance patterns for the CF gene are shown in the accompanying diagram. Each child, whether male or female, has a 25 percent risk of inheriting a defective gene from each parent and of having CF. A child born to two CF patients (an unlikely event) would be at a 100 percent risk of developing CF. The presence of two mutant genes (g) is needed for CF to appear. Each parent carries one defective gene (g) and one normal gene (G). The single normal gene is sufficient for normal function of the mucus glands, and the parents are therefore CF-free. Each child has a 25 percent risk of inheriting two defective genes and getting CF, a 25 percent chance of inheriting two normal genes, and a 50 percent chance of being an unaffected carrier like the parents.

Safety

Preventing accidents, especially automobile accidents, is of utmost importance. There are several things you can do to help prevent accidents, including driving sober, obeying traffic laws, using your safety belt and being aware of other drivers. Alcohol was present in 37% of all traffic accidents with fatalities. Be sober before driving or use a designated driver.

Most car accidents occur within a mile of a person's home. In this area people are more familiar with the area and feel less of a need to pay attention. There are also more children in a residential area which adds to the risk.

Equipment failure, roadway design, and poor roadway maintenance are all factors involved in vehicular accidents. However, at least 60% of accidents can be blamed primarily on the driver. Driving distracted, drowsy, and drunk, are all problems that are the drivers fault, and are likely to cause accidents. Driving distracted, such as playing loud music, talking to passengers or texting, takes the driver's attention off of the road, making them more likely to miss something and cause an accident. Similar problems come from driving drowsy.

Be careful in your own home and watch children. Falls account for the highest rate of accidental death in the home. If an accident, in the home, at school or elsewhere occurs, you may need to know first aid and apply it. You can become certified in first aid by the American Red Cross. They can also certify you to perform CPR.

When someone stops breathing:

1. Check responsiveness by trying to get the victim to talk to you
2. Dial 911
3. Look, listen and feel for breath and/or chest movement
4. Open the airway by tilting the victim's head back
5. Look, listen and feel for breath and/or chest movement
6. Give two slow breaths
7. Look, listen and feel for breath and/or chest movement
8. Check for pulse
9. Continue as instructed by authorities or until they arrive

When someone is choking, perform the Heimlich maneuver to remove whatever is lodged in the throat, preventing breathing.

1. Wrap your arms around the victim's waist and make a fist with one hand
2. Place fist near the belly button, well below the sternum
3. Cover your fist with your other hand
4. Press fist into abdomen with other hand with five quick upward thrusts
5. After every five thrusts check victim and placement of fist if you need to repeat

Fire Safety

While the best way to deal with fire situations is prevention, there are some strategies which will increase a person's chances of getting out safely if they are stuck in a fire and can't get out. First, stay low. Smoke rises, which means the air near the floor will be cleaner than the air at standing level. Second, be aware of your surroundings. Before opening any doors, notice if there is smoke coming from the other side. If there is, don't open it. Also, feel to see if the area seems hotter, because if so there's probably fire on the other side of the door. Don't just grab on to door handles, because if there is a fire on the other side the metal will heat up. Third, call for help as best as possible. Try to find a window or other opening if possible.

Consumerism

Advertisers of health care products and services use marketing tactics to get your attention and sell you their products. Claims can seem to be supported by cases of spontaneous remission or the placebo effect (symptoms disappearing because you believe they should). Self-care and responsibility for one's health are critical in reducing rising health care concerns and costs. Allopathic or traditional medicine is based on scientifically validated methods and procedures. Concerns in the U.S. healthcare field include cost, access to skilled practitioners, fraud, and malpractice. Health insurance is becoming more and more expensive. The business concept behind health insurance is calculating the risk factors within a large group of people.

For example, a healthy patient will pay the same premium and may never need to be hospitalized as a non-healthy patient, who will pay the same premium (usually in addition to a deductible) but will be hospitalized to receive expensive treatments.

Managed care programs or HMOs attempt to keep costs lower by streamlining administrative processes and pressing preventative care.

Another way consumers are keeping their premiums as low as possible is to choose high deductible insurance plans.

In a typical insurance scenario, you pay a monthly amount per person for medical coverage. For this example, let's say it is $300 per month. If you broke your leg, your insurance would cover you on an 80/20 split. Meaning, your insurance would pay 80% of your medical expenses and you would pay 20%. However, you have to pay your deductible first. This might be $1000, $2500 or as high as $10,000. A deductible is the amount you must pay first, out of pocket, before your insurance pays their portion.

Your fees were:

1. Dr. Visit $150
2. X-rays $300
3. Casting $500
4. Physical Therapy $500

Total $1450

If your deductible was only $1000, you would pay your doctor's the first $1000. Then your insurance would cover the remaining $450 at 80%. So they would pay $360 and you would pay $90.

If your deductible was $2500, you would pay the entire amount of your bill. Your deductible restarts every calendar year, so after you meet the deductible threshold, you are there until January 1, when you would have to begin again.

Because high deductible plans are so much cheaper, many consumers are opting for this insurance. This is also sometimes referred to as catastrophic insurance plans because it won't cover small things like broken bones or the flu but will cover a car accident, cancer, emergency surgery, etc. Have a plan like this is better than no insurance at all because a major surgery or accident would bankrupt most consumers that don't have any insurance.

Environmental Concerns

Population experts believe that the most challenging environmental issue today is to slow the population growth of the world. However, the population growth is not distributed equally around the world. In less developed countries, populations double every 10 to 15 years and overwhelm their government's ability to provide the basic necessities.

Air pollution is another health concern. The major air pollutants are:

- Sulfur Dioxide: by-product of fossil fuels, i.e. smelters, refineries
- Particulates: cigarette smoke and some industrial uses
- Carbon Monoxide: odorless gas primarily from automobile emissions
- Nitrogen Dioxide: from coal powered boilers
- Ozone
- Lead: metal pollutant found in old paint, pipes, etc.

These six pollutants are regulated by the Clean Air Act. There are also now several hybrid cars on the market which emit fewer fossil fuels, helping to reduce air pollution.

Acid rain is rain that has fallen through acidic air or polluted air and becomes polluted. CFCs or Cholorflurocarbons are chemicals that contribute to the depletion of the ozone layer. CFCs were found in aerosols and Styrofoam but when it was determined that they caused damage to the ozone layer, they were banned in the U.S. and now in over 160 countries.

The ozone layer is what keeps us safe from Ultraviolet B rays from the sun. It helps prevent skin cancer and global warming. Global warming is a result of the greenhouse effect, when gases such as carbon monoxide and methane become a layer surrounding the earth that lets in the heat from the sun but traps it near the earth's surface.

In the United States, the agency in charge of enforcing water quality standards is the Environmental Protection Agency, or EPA. This agency is responsible for the protection of the environment and humans in enforcing legislation passed by Congress.

The EPA is over a number of different areas including the quality of drinking water, protection of endangered species, hazardous waste, and air quality.

There is also pollution that can occur underwater, in our lakes and oceans. Besides the regular concerns of accidental oils spills, some companies dump their waste in water, contaminating it for fish, other wildlife, etc. This can sometimes leach into the ground water, poisoning water for entire towns.

Another type of pollution that occurs underwater is underwater noise pollution also called underwater acoustic pollution. Because animals such as whales use high frequency sonar in order to navigate and locate prey, interference and added noise can confuse and harm them. A simplified view of this is tapping on the fish tank in the doctor's office. The noise does in fact scare the fish and on a large scale is a threat to marine life.

Sample Test Questions

1) Divergent thinking in psychology is

 A) Focusing on a finite number of solutions rather than proposing multiple solutions
 B) Systematic and logical thinking
 C) Thought process or method used to generate creative ideas
 D) A carefully prepared step by step process thinking

The correct answer is: C:) Thought process or method used to generate creative ideas. Divergent thinking refers to a way of solving problems wherein a variety of possible solutions are looked into in an effort to find one that works for every individual.

2) Having Syphilis or German measles in a pregnancy is most dangerous at the stage of

 A) 5 weeks
 B) 10 weeks
 C) 20 weeks
 D) 30 weeks

The correct answer is: C:) 20 weeks. German measles (Rubella) and Syphilis are most dangerous to a baby if the mother catches it during the first 20 weeks of pregnancy. It can cause miscarriage, stillbirth or birth defects. While in unborn babies, the possible dangers hearing loss and brain damage.

3) Dialectical perspective means

 A) A social, political, or material inequality of a social group
 B) Dialect is registered early, automatically, and in parallel
 C) Society is a complex system who works together to promote solidarity
 D) An assumption of that all social relationships are interwoven with multiple contradictions

The correct answer is: D:) An assumption of that all social relationships are interwoven with multiple contradictions. The most important assumption of social dialectical theories is that all relationships such as friendships, romantic relationships and family relationship are interconnected with multiple contradictions. Social dialectics is not a single theory but a family of theories.

4) Carrol Gilligan's theory of moral development for women has three major divisions: pre-conventional, conventional and post conventional. These transitions she believed are fueled by a changes of what?

    A) Change of self
    B) Change of cognitive capability
    C) Change of environment
    D) Change of beliefs

The correct answer is: A:) Change of self. According to Gilligan, women can gain personal independence after they forget about their role is for other people alone. In our society, women really invest in helping other people, however, they should care about themselves as much as they do about others for their own benefits as well.

5) What is the active chemical in Marijuana?

    A) PCP
    B) LSD
    C) THC
    D) MDMA

The correct answer is C:) THC. The main active chemical is THC (delta-9-tetrahydrocannabinol).

6) What are antigens?

    A) Cells in the blood stream which help strengthen the veins.
    B) Anything which triggers a response from the immune system.
    C) Something created by B cells to protect the body from infection.
    D) Substances in the body which help fight pathogens.

The correct answer is B:) Anything which triggers a response from the immune system. Answers C and D both refer to antibodies.

7) Gastroenteritis is

    A) A severe pain in the stomach
    B) A functioning of pancreatic juices in the duodenum
    C) A functioning of pancreatic juices in the stomach
    D) An inability to swallow

The correct answer is B:) A functioning of pancreatic juices in the duodenum. Gastroenteritis occurs when the pancreatic juices begin functioning in the duodenum, the opening to the stomach.

8) The duodenum is:

A) The large intestine
B) An extension of the lungs
C) The opening of the rectum
D) The opening to the stomach

The correct answer is D:) The opening to the stomach.

9) Which of the following is NOT an example of active immunization?

A) Transferring already made antibodies to another person.
B) Contracting a disease and building up antibodies to fight it.
C) Getting a vaccination to build up immunity to a disease.
D) When a child gets chickenpox, and never gets them again.

The correct answer is A:) Transferring already made antibodies to another person. This is an example of passive immunization.

10) Which of the following is the Black Plague an example of?

A) A disease which made people's hair turn black
B) A pandemic
C) An epidemic
D) A slave rebellion

The correct answer is B:) A pandemic. The Black Plague quickly spread across Europe, giving it a large spread, and killed millions of people.

11) What does MMR stand for?

A) Measles, mumps, and rubella
B) Measles, malaria, and rubella
C) Measles, mumps, and retinitis
D) Mumps, measles and rheumatism

The correct answer is A:) Measles, mumps, and rubella. MMR refers to measles, mumps, and rubella.

12) What is an ischemic stroke?

A) When the blood vessels leading to the brain start flowing to quickly.
B) When there is a clot or other type of blockage in an artery leading to the brain.
C) When a person's blood vessels don't close off, and blood begins to flow backwards.
D) Scientists aren't really sure what it is, only that it is common.

The correct answer is B:) When there is a clot or other type of blockage leading to the brain.

13) What is the purpose of platelets?

A) To make blood flow through the veins smoothly.
B) Platelets help thicken the blood so that it doesn't flow through the veins to quickly.
C) The main function of platelets is to stop bleeding by clotting.
D) Platelets help filter the blood.

The correct answer is C:) The main function of platelets is to stop bleeding by clotting.

14) The causes for cancer are

A) Race
B) Exposure to chemicals
C) From sun exposure
D) Largely unknown

The correct answer is D:) Largely unknown. The causes of cancer are speculated and are largely unknown.

15) What does MVP stand for?

A) Mitral Valve Prolapse
B) Mitral Valve Pressure
C) Marfan Valve Prolapse
D) Marfan Valve Pressure

The correct answer is A:) Mitral Valve Prolapse.

16) Arrhythmia refers to:

A) Rapid heart beat
B) Slow heart beat
C) Irregular heart beat
D) Undetectable heart beat

The correct answer is C:) Irregular heartbeat. An arrhythmia is an irregular heart beat.

17) The cardiovascular system refers to:

A) The lungs
B) The heart
C) The kidneys
D) The liver

The correct answer is B:) The heart. The cardiovascular refers to the heart and pumping of blood.

18) What is the technical term for the body's response to stress?

A) Eustress
B) Distress
C) General Adaptation Syndrome
D) None of the above

The correct answer is C:) General Adaptation Syndrome. Eustress and distress are two different types of stress, however General Adaptation Syndrome is the term for the body's response to stress.

19) The U.S. Government's Health Center

A) Recommends chickenpox vaccines for all babies
B) Recommends vaccinations for babies two weeks after birth
C) Recommends that teenagers and adults, not previously vaccinated, should have two injections one week apart
D) Recommends vaccinations for all ages

The correct answer is D:) Recommends vaccinations for all ages. The United States guidelines recommend that everyone who has not had the disease be vaccinated.

20) What is the daily recommended dose of aspirin to reduce the risk of heart attack?

A) 65 mg
B) 75 mg
C) 80 mg
D) 85 mg

The correct answer is B:) 75 mg.

21) Which of the follow does alcoholism NOT increase the chances of?

A) Liver failure
B) Living a long life
C) Heart disease
D) Brain damage

The correct answer is B:) Living a long life. Alcoholism decreases a person's life expectancy, not the other way around.

22) Which of the following is NOT a possible description of diabetes?

A) The pancreas does not produce sufficient insulin.
B) The liver, muscle, and fat cells do not respond normally to insulin.
C) Answers A and B are both possible descriptions of diabetes.
D) Free radicals in the body damage cells, and cause them to die.

The correct answer is D:) Free radicals in the body damage cells, and cause them to die. This is a description of the Free Radical Theory of Aging. Answers A and B both describe diabetes. Answer C is correct, but does not answer the question.

23) What is considered binge drinking?

A) Having 3 drinks in quick succession
B) Having 4 drinks in quick succession
C) Having 5 drinks in quick succession
D) Having 6 drinks in quick succession

The correct answer is C:) Having 5 drinks in quick succession.

24) Measles

A) Is not contagious
B) Typically runs for five days
C) Begins as a respiratory disease
D) Is contagious when the first of the rash appears

The correct answer is C:) Begins as a respiratory disease. Measles begins as a respiratory infection.

25) What are essential amino acids?

A) The 20 amino acids which the body needs to function properly.
B) The 9 amino acids which the body does not produce itself.
C) The 11 amino acids which the body is able to produce itself.
D) Another name for amino acids in general, because they are so essential to life.

The correct answer is B:) The 9 amino acids which the body does not produce itself.

26) The first step in caring for a measles patient is:

A) Reduce the fever
B) Apply Non-itch cream to the rash
C) Take the infected person to the doctor
D) Give aspirin

The correct answer is A:) Reduce the fever. It is important to first reduce the fever.

27) What is a complete protein?

A) A protein built by the body which has all 20 of the amino acids.
B) A food which contains all 11 of the amino acids which the body produces.
C) A food which contains all 20 of the amino acids necessary for the body to function.
D) A food which contains all 9 of the essential amino acids.

The correct answer is D:) A food which contains all 9 of the essential amino acids.

28) What type of cells does Human Immunodeficiency Virus (HIV) attack?

A) Helper T Cells
B) Cytotoxic T Cells
C) Memory B Cells
D) Memory T Cells

The correct answer is A:) Helper T Cells. Helper T cells are important because they signal the B cells to make antigens, and activate the cytotoxic T cells.

29) In which stage does the body repair damage caused by the infection?

A) Convalescence
B) Prodromal
C) Invasive
D) Incubation

The correct answer is A:) Convalescence. Convalescence is the final stage of infection. It is now that the body returns to health and repairs damage.

30) How can having too many platelets in the blood cause problems?

A) The blood gets really thick, causing fatigue.
B) The blood won't clot over a cut, and it will keep bleeding.
C) The body will stop making red blood cells because it thinks there is already enough blood.
D) The blood can clot when it isn't supposed to, which could cause a stroke or other problem.

The correct answer is D:) The blood can clot when it isn't supposed to, which could cause a stroke or other problem. Answer B would be true of having too few platelets in the blood.

31) The 3 C's accompanying measles are:

A) Cough, Coryza, and Conjunctivitis.
B) Cough, Cholera, and Coryza.
C) Cough, Carcinoma Catharsis.
D) Cough, Carcinogens, Coryza

The correct answer is A:) Cough, Coryza, and Conjunctivitis. The Three Cs of measles are Cough, Coryza, and Conjunctivitis.

32) The salivary glands are located

A) In the ears
B) In the chest
C) Inside the cheeks
D) On the face

The correct answer is C:) Inside the cheeks. The salivary glands are those that produce saliva.

33) What is the most common type of stroke?

A) Subarachnoid Hemorrhage
B) Intracerebral Hemorrhage
C) Ischemic Stroke
D) All types of strokes are equally likely to occur

The correct answer is C:) Ischemic Stroke. This is when there is blockage to arteries leading to the brain.

34) Which of the following is NOT true of congestive heart failure?

A) It is characterized by the heart suddenly "failing."
B) Nausea, fatigue, and swelling in the ankles and legs are all symptoms of congestive heart failure.
C) Decreased blood flow to the kidney causes it to filter less fluid out of the blood.
D) The heart doesn't circulate a sufficient amount of blood through the system.

This correct answer is A:) It is characterized by the heart suddenly "failing." Congestive heart failure is when the heart isn't circulating enough blood, but it is still working.

35) Mumps are

A) Recognizable by a severe rash on the face
B) Recognizable by swelling of glands in the neck
C) Not contagious
D) Usually preceded by both fever and chills

The correct answer is B:) Recognizable by swelling of glands in the neck. The evidence of mumps is the swelling of neck glands.

36) Which of the following does NOT offer support to the Theory of Programmed Aging?

A) The body has the ability to repair itself.
B) Members of the same species tend to die around the same age.
C) Overweight people have shorter lifespans.
D) Some species die suddenly after reproduction.

The correct answer is C:) Overweight people have shorter lifespans. This answer indicates that it is lifestyle that determines lifespan, which does not agree with the Theory of Programmed Aging.

37) Which of the following is a type of cardiomyopathy?

A) Hypertrophic cardiomyopathy
B) Congestive cardiomyopathy
C) Neither A or B
D) Both A and B are types of cardiomyopathy

The correct answer is D:) Both A and B are types of cardiomyopathy. Hypertrophic cardiomyopathy is hardening of heart tissue, and congestive cardiomyopathy is weakening of the heart.

38) Angina refers to:

A) Chest pain
B) Irregular heart beat
C) Heart attack
D) Pain in left arm

The correct answer is A:) Chest pain. Angina is chest pain and may be followed by a heart attack.

39) Which of the following is TRUE?

A) Transferring already made antibodies to another person is passive immunization.
B) Vaccination is one type of passive immunization.
C) When a person gets sick and their body develops antibodies to fight the infection, it is passive immunization because they didn't actively try to immunize themselves before getting sick.
D) Transferring already made antibodies to another person is active immunization.

The correct answer is A:) Transferring already made antibodies to another person is passive immunization. Active immunization is any case in which antigens are introduced into a person's system. This can include getting sick or vaccinated.

40) What is the most common assisted reproduction method?

A) In vitro fertilization
B) Various types of surgery
C) Surrogate mothers
D) All methods are equally used

The correct answer is A:) In vitro fertilization. Technically in vitro fertilization is a type of surgery, but Answer B is too vague to be considered correct in this sense.

41) Government statistics about the rate of heart attacks tell us:

A) 1.2 million heart attacks occur each year
B) 1.5 thousand heart attacks occur each year
C) An unknown number of hearts attacks occur each year
D) Several thousand heart attacks occur each year

The correct answer is A:) 1.2 million heart attacks occur each year.

42) Which one of the following statements is TRUE?

A) More men than women develop heart disease
B) More women than men develop heart disease
C) The number of men and the number of women who develop heart disease is about equal
D) While the numbers are changing, more men than women still develop heart disease

The correct answer is D:) While the numbers are changing, more men than women still develop heart disease. The number of women suffering heart attacks is growing annually.

43) What group is most affect by sickle cell disease?

A) Pacific Islanders
B) Hispanics
C) Caucasians
D) African Americans

The correct answer is D:) African Americans. About 1 of every 600 African American children inherit this disease.

44) Is it possible to get protein from non-animal sources?

A) No, because only animals are able to produce amino acids.
B) No, because the body isn't capable of combining amino acids from different foods.
C) Yes, because plants can make complete proteins too.
D) Yes, because the body is capable of combining amino acids from different foods.

The correct answer is D:) Yes, because the body is capable of combining amino acids from different foods. While C is a correct response, it is an incorrect statement because plants do not make complete proteins.

45) Which of the following is NOT true of trans fat?

A) Trans fat is more solid than oil, so it makes it feel less greasy.
B) Trans fat is used to give food a longer shelf life.
C) Trans fat is oily, and is an ingredient in many greasy foods.
D) Trans fat is considered one of the worst types of fats.

The correct answer is C:) Trans fat is oily, and is an ingredient in many greasy foods. Trans fat is more solid than oil.

46) Which one of the following statements is correct?

A) Having a family history of heart disease makes you less likely to develop heart disease
B) Having a family history makes you more likely to develop heart disease
C) Your family history has no bearing on your likelihood to develop heart disease
D) Your race does not have any bearing on the risk for heart disease

The correct answer is B:) Having a family history makes you more likely to develop heart disease. Family history is definitely a risk factor in your likelihood to develop heart disease.

47) Which of the following should a person do during a fire?

A) Keep quiet so you don't distract the fire fighters who are looking for you from their search.
B) Check to see if a door is hot before opening it.
C) Don't sit down because they hair higher up is better for breathing.
D) Find all of your favorite things before trying to get out so they don't get burned in the fire.

The correct answer is B:) Check to see if a door is hot before opening it. If it is hot there is likely a fire on the other side.

48) Which of the following is NOT true of sickle cells disease?

A) The irregular shape in the blood cells causes the blood to flow smoother.
B) Sickle cell disease can also be called sickle cell anemia.
C) Sickle Hemoglobin is the name for the irregular hemoglobin of sickle cell disease.
D) People with sickle cell disease have twisted and rigid blood cells.

The correct answer is A:) The irregular shape in the blood cells causes the blood to flow smoother. The irregular shape causes problems with blood flow, which can result in organ damage.

49) Which of the following is NOT an example of an epidemic?

A) The predicted flu rate in Los Angeles was 15%, however 45% of the city got sick.
B) It was expected that 10% of the people at the high school would get sick. However, 40% of the student body called in sick the next week.
C) An outbreak in 1918 of the Spanish Influenza spread worldwide and killed an estimated 50 million people (3% of the world's population), and an estimated 500 million people were infected.
D) After one of the guards got sick, it was expected that around 12% of the prison inmates would get sick, however it actually ended up being around 50%.

The correct answer is C:) An outbreak in 1918 of the Spanish Influenza spread world-wide and killed an estimated 50 million people (3% of the world's population), and an estimated 500 million people were infected. This is a pandemic, not an epidemic, because it spread worldwide.

50) Men are __________ more likely to die from suicide then women.

A) 2 times
B) 3 times
C) 4 times
D) 5 times

The correct answer is C:) 4 times. Men are four times more likely than women to die from suicide. However, three times more women than men report attempting suicide.

51) What is osteoarthritis?

A) A type of autoimmune disease.
B) A disease where a person's skin begins to harden.
C) The gradual deterioration of bones and joints.
D) A rare form of heart failure.

The correct answer is C:) The gradual deterioration of bones and joints.

52) What is the holistic approach to medicine?

A) Various factors in a person's life can have an effect on their overall health.
B) The body's health is the only thing related to a person's overall health.
C) There is no such thing as holistic health, it isn't a real term.
D) Both A and B are possible descriptions of the holistic approach to medicine.

The correct answer is A:) Various factors in a person's life can have an effect on their overall health.

53) Which one of the following statements is correct?

A) Being overweight is not a risk factor for developing heart disease as long as you are physically active
B) Being overweight at the waistline is a potential risk factor for developing heart disease
C) "Overweight" can only be defined by the individual
D) Being overweight is not a risk factor for heart disease as long as you are happy

The correct answer is B:) Being overweight at the waistline is a potential risk factor for developing heart disease. Being overweight is a risk factor for developing heart disease. Excess fat at the waistline is the most dangerous factor of all.

54) How does the body obtain nutrients?

A) Through the respiratory process
B) Through the digestion process
C) Through the food chain
D) Through contact with the air

The correct answer is B:) Through the digestion process. The respiratory process has to do with breathing, not eating.

55) Why are multiple sclerosis and the Epstein-Barr virus thought to be related?

A) Because people with MS have higher numbers of antibodies for EBV than expected.
B) Because every person who ever had MS also had EBV.
C) They aren't; the two diseases have nothing to do with each other.
D) Because EBV weakens the immune system making it highly susceptible to MS.

The correct answer is A:) Because people with MS have higher numbers of antibodies for EBV than expected.

56) Which of the following is NOT a category of plant made proteins?

A) Dairy
B) Legumes
C) Grains
D) Seeds and nuts

The correct answer is A:) Dairy. Legumes, grains, and seeds and nuts are all categories of plant made proteins.

57) BMI refers to:

A) Body Measurement Index
B) Body Midriff Index
C) Body Mass Index
D) Brain Mass Index

The correct answer is C:) Body Mass Index. Body Mass Index is important to compute your mass vs. fat.

58) According to the holistic approach, which of the following affects overall health?

A) Stress level
B) Family relationships
C) Work conditions
D) All of the above

The correct answer is D:) All of the above. The holistic approach is the belief that many different aspects of a person's life affect their overall health.

59) How much of the energy that a person consumes is used without them doing anything?

A) 40%
B) 50%
C) 60%
D) 70%

The correct answer is D:) 70%.

60) Hypertension relates to:

A) Stress level
B) Excitability
C) Blood pressure
D) Anger management level

The correct answer is C:) Blood pressure. Hypertension is the medical name for high blood pressure.

61) The early symptoms of Alzheimer's disease are often confused with which disorder?

A) Depression
B) Bipolar
C) Heart Failure
D) Down Syndrome

The correct answer is A:) Depression. They share symptoms such as personality changes, lack of interest in previously enjoyed activities, and forgetfulness.

62) What is the maximum heart rate for a person who is 40 years old?

A) 200 bmp
B) 180 bmp
C) 160 bmp
D) 220 bmp

The correct answer is B:) 180 bmp. The maximum heart rate is found by subtracting the person's age, in this case 40, from 220. 220-40=180 bmp.

63) A blood pressure report is in two numbers, e.g., 120/65. Systolic refers to:

A) The upper number of a fraction
B) The upper or first number of a blood pressure reading
C) Pulse rate
D) The bottom number of a blood pressure reading

The correct answer is B:) The upper or first number of a blood pressure reading. Systolic refers to the upper number of a blood pressure reading.

64) The bottom number of a blood pressure reading is called:

A) Denominator
B) Numerator
C) Diastolic
D) Pressure at rest

The correct answer is C:) Diastolic. The bottom number of a blood pressure reading is the diastolic.

65) What percent of a person's maximum heart rate is their target heart rate?

A) 60%-80%
B) 50%-60%
C) 40%-50%
D) 70%-90%

The correct answer is A:) 60%-80%.

66) What is cremation?

A) A South American country.
B) Burying a person's body after they have died.
C) A delicacy native to India.
D) Burning a dead person's remains.

The correct answer is D:) Burning a dead person's remains.

67) Diabetics should:

A) Keep their sugar level under control to lower the risk of heart disease
B) Realize that they are not at risk for heart disease
C) Maintain careful eating habits but not worry about heart disease
D) Keep their sugar level under control at all times to lessen the risk of heart disease

The correct answer is D:) Keep their sugar level under control at all times to lessen the risk of heart disease. Diabetes is definitely a risk factor for heart disease. It is important that the sugar level be controlled at all times.

68) What does LDL stand for?

A) Low Degree Lipid-proteins
B) Low Degree Lipoproteins
C) Low Density Lipid-proteins
D) Low Density Lipoproteins

The correct answer is D:) Low Density Lipoproteins.

69) What is the most common form of arthritis?

A) Osteoarthritis
B) Rheumatoid Arthritis
C) Fibromyalgia
D) All types of arthritis are equally likely to occur

The correct answer is A:) Osteoarthritis. Osteoarthritis is the gradual deterioration of bones and joints.

70) What is a living will?

A) A document in which a person outlines what they want to be done for medical treatment.
B) A document in which a person states who they want to make medical decisions for them.
C) A document in which a person dictates what will be done with their possessions when they die.
D) "Living will" is not an actual term.

The correct answer is A:) A document in which a person outlines what they want to be done for medical treatment. Answer B describes a health proxy.

71) A healthy blood pressure reading should not exceed

A) 230/85
B) 110/60
C) 130/80
D) The upper limits of a safe blood pressure are 140 over 90

The correct answer is D:) The upper limits of a safe blood pressure are 140 over 90. Blood pressures over 140 and under 90 call for immediate attention.

72) Which one of the following statements is correct?

A) A sedentary lifestyle is a risk factor in heart disease
B) A sedentary lifestyle is recommended for heart disease patients
C) A sedentary lifestyle is synonymous with a physically active lifestyle
D) A sedentary lifestyle risk factor for heart disease

The correct answer is A:) A sedentary lifestyle is a risk factor in heart disease. An active lifestyle, within your physical limitations, is important in preventing heart disease.

73) Which of the following statements is correct?

A) Diabetes is a risk factor for heart disease
B) Controlled diabetes is not a risk factor for heart disease
C) A person's response to stress can be a risk factor for heart disease
D) It is good to "Blow your top"; it clears the air and relaxes you

The correct answer is C:) A person's response to stress can be a risk factor for heart disease. How a person responds to stress either reduces or increases the risk of heart disease.

74) Which of the following is NOT true of Multiple Sclerosis?

A) The abbreviation for Multiple Sclerosis is MS.
B) Multiple sclerosis usually begins to show around the age of 25.
C) The symptoms always come on quickly.
D) MS can cause paralysis.

The correct answer is C:) The symptoms always come on quickly. The symptoms of MS usually come on gradually, with periods of remission between periods of worsening.

75) Which of the following is NOT a true statement?

A) Nausea and vomiting are possible side effects of abortion.
B) Vaginal bleeding is a possible side effect of abortion.
C) Abdominal swelling is a possible side effect of abortion.
D) Abortion has no side effects.

The correct answer is D:) Abortion has no side effects. Abortion has many possible side effects.

76) Which of the following is NOT a suspected cause of schizophrenia?

A) Genetics
B) Reduced gray matter tissue
C) Heart problems
D) Increased amounts of neurotransmitters

The correct answer is C:) Heart problems. Schizophrenia is a mental disease, and genetics, reduced gray matter tissue, and increased amounts of neurotransmitters are all suspected causes.

77) Physical activity

A) Helps to reduce the risk factor of heart disease
B) Must be strenuous to be helpful
C) Need not be scheduled to reduce the risk of heart disease
D) Is too difficult for the average person

The correct answer is A:) Helps to reduce the risk factor of heart disease. Physical activity helps reduce the risk of heart disease.

78) Injuries from physical activity:

A) Happen to everyone
B) Generally happen to those who have been inactive for a period of time
C) Happen only to others
D) Often happens when in inactive person does not gradually work up to an exercise routine

The correct answer is D:) Often happens when in inactive person does not gradually work up to an exercise. An exercise routine should be worked into gradually.

79) A heart-healthy diet

A) Avoids fried food
B) Requires that you eliminate all fried foods
C) Reduces sodium intake
D) Does not affect your cholesterol

The correct answer is C:) Reduces sodium intake. Reducing salt intake is one factor in lowering the risk of heart disease.

80) What infection does Gardasil protect against?

A) HPV
B) MVP
C) HCG
D) IVF

The correct answer is A:) HPV. Human papilloma virus.

81) Abdominal pressure is a symptom of heart disease

A) For men
B) For women
C) For children
D) For everyone

The correct answer is B:) For women. Abdominal pressure is a possible symptom for women.

82) The level of exercise should be determined by

A) Age
B) Physical condition
C) Both age and condition
D) Ambition

The correct answer is C:) Both age and condition. Any exercise routine should be based on both factors.

83) Blushing is an example of what?

A) General Adaptation Syndrome
B) A virus
C) Vasocongestion
D) There is no term which applies to blushing

The correct answer is C:) Vasocongestion. Vasocongestion is when there is increased blood flow to a specific area.

84) Smoking cigarettes is

A) A serious risk factor for most cancers
B) Not harmful if done in moderation
C) Not a serious risk factor for many diseases
D) Relaxes the smokers brain function

The correct answer is A:) A serious risk factor for most cancers. Cigarette smoking of any amount is harmful to the body and is known to cause cancer.

85) What is the main difference between a living will and a health proxy?

A) There is no different between a living will and a health proxy. They both refer to the same thing.
B) A living will dictates another person to make medical decisions, while a heath proxy states the patient's wishes.
C) Living will and health proxy are both incorrect terms.
D) A health proxy dictates another person to make medical decisions, while a living will states the patient's wishes.

The correct answer is D:) A health proxy dictates another person to make medical decisions, while a living will states the patient's wishes. Answer B is close, however it switches the two terms around.

86) Where do most traffic accidents occur?

A) When people are on vacation
B) Within 10 miles of a person's home
C) Within 1 mile of a person's home
D) Within 1 mile of a person's workplace

The correct answer is C:) Within 1 mile of a person's home.

87) A CVA is

A) Chronic vaginal activity
B) Cardiovascular accident
C) Curable vascular activity
D) Complete vascular attack

The correct answer is B:) Cardiovascular accident.

88) What is the term for decreased function of the heart?

A) Mitral valve prolapse
B) Cardiomyopathy
C) Vasocongestion
D) Sickle Cell Disease

The correct answer is B:) Cardiomyopathy.

89) One of the preventative steps a person should take for heart disease is:

A) Cut down on the number of cigarettes smoked per day
B) Smoke cigars
C) Smoke only in private to avoid disseminating secondhand smoke
D) Quit smoking

The correct answer is D:) Quit smoking. Stop all tobacco use.

90) Which of the following describes in vitro fertilization?

A) A woman takes special medicine to increase her chances of getting pregnant.
B) An agreement in which a woman agrees to bear a child to be raised by others.
C) An egg cell is a combined with a sperm cell in a laboratory where it develops into an embryo.
D) There is no such thing as in vitro fertilization. It is only an untested theory.

The correct answer is C:) An egg cell is a combined with a sperm cell in a laboratory where it develops into an embryo.

91) What factor is to blame for 60% of all vehicular accidents?

A) Equipment failure
>B) Driver behavior
C) Roadway design
D) Poor roadway maintenance

The correct answer is B:) Driver behavior. Driving distracted and drowsy are examples of poor driving habits.

92) To help prevent heart disease, you should:

>A) Avoid stressful situations
B) Avoid outbursts of anger; keep it all inside
C) "Sound off" later
D) Allow your anger to simmer

The correct answer is A:) Avoid stressful situations.

93) Alcohol

>A) May be consumed in moderation
B) Is bad for you in any amount
C) Should be limited to an occasional binge
D) Should be limited to 3 drinks daily for men; 2, for women

The correct answer is A:) May be consumer in moderation. The recommended levels are 2 drinks for men; 1 drink for women.

94) What government agency enforces water quality standards?

A) ACF
>B) EPA
C) FAA
D) FCC

The correct answer is B:) EPA. EPA stands for the Environmental Protection Agency.

95) Which of the following is NOT a benefit of regular exercise?

A) Antidepressant
B) Decreased risk of certain diseases
C) Weight gain
D) Increases neuron production

The correct answer is C:) Weight gain. Answers A, B, and C are all positive effects of regular exercise.

96) Perfusion is

A) The spreading of a body disease
B) Distributing widely
C) The passing of fluid
D) Severe confusion

The correct answer is B:) Distributing widely.

97) Which of the following describes the Wear and Tear Theory of Aging?

A) Free radicals in the body cause damage to cells.
B) As damage to the body accumulates, the body learns better how to deal with problems and gets stronger.
C) As damage to the body accumulates, body systems wear out.
D) A person who has liver failure has it because their cells were programmed to stop working at a certain time.

The correct answer is C:) As damage to the body accumulates, body systems wear out. Answer A describes the Free Radical Theory of Aging, and Answer D describes the Theory of Programmed Aging.

98) Which of the following correctly lists the stages of dying in order?

A) Denial, Anger, Bargaining, Depression, and Acceptance
B) Bargaining, Anger, Denial, Acceptance, and Depression
C) Anger, Acceptance, Depression, Denial, and Bargaining
D) Denial, Bargaining, Anger, Depression, and Acceptance

The correct answer is A:) Denial, Anger, Bargaining, Depression, and Acceptance. Answer D comes close, however it reverses bargaining and anger.

99) What is the life expectancy of alcoholics compared to the rest of the population?

A) 10-12 years less
B) 10-12 years more
C) 5-6 years less
D) 14-15 years less

The correct answer is A:) 10-12 years less.

100) Strokes are

A) The number 1 killer
B) The number 2 killer
C) The number 3 killer
D) Behind heart, cancer, and emphysema deaths

The correct answer is C:) The number 3 killer. Strokes are the No. 3 killer behind heart disease and cancer.

101) A symptom of a stroke is:

A) A one-sided droop of the face
B) Clear speech
C) The ability to repeat a sentence
D) A fever

The correct answer is A:) A one-sided droop of the face.

102) If you suspect a person is having a stroke,

A) Check for breathing
B) Check for pulse
C) Move objects out of the way
D) Call 9-1-1

The correct answer is D:) Call 9-1-1. Time is critical. Call 9-1-1 or take the person to the hospital immediately.

103) Which of the following is an example of a benign tumor?

A) Breast cancer
B) A mole
C) Liver cancer
D) Colon cancer

The correct answer is B:) A mole. Breast cancer, liver cancer, and colon cancer are all examples of cancers which form malignant tumors.

104) About how fast does the average person's liver metabolize alcohol at?

A) .6 oz per hour
B) 6 oz per hour
C) .6 mL per hour
D) 6 mL per hour

The correct answer is A:) .6 oz per hour.

105) A TIA is:

A) A sudden, short stroke
B) Transmission of infected agents
C) A shower
D) Leakage of body fluid

The correct answer is A:) A sudden, short stroke.

106) Which of the following statements supports the Free Radical Theory of Aging?

A) A person's lifestyle determines their lifespan.
B) Free radicals in the body cause damage to cells.
C) A person's liver cells are programmed to automatically stop working after 72 years.
D) People die in car crashes.

The correct answer is B:) Free radicals in the body cause damage to cells. Answers A and D both support the Wear and Tear Theory of Aging. Answer C describes the Theory of Programmed Aging.

107) The most critical factor in treatment when a stroke occurs is

A) Calling the doctor
B) Wasting no time
C) Placing the patient in a prone position
D) Talking to patient to put the patient at ease

The correct answer is B:) Wasting no time. Waste no time is getting help. If possible, note the time the patient suffered the stroke. The doctor or ER will need that information.

108) Which of the following is NOT a symptom of congestive heart failure?

A) Shortness of breath due to buildup of fluid in the lungs.
B) Nausea due to buildup of fluid in the liver.
C) Inability to sleep while sitting up.
D) Fatigue because less oxygen is circulating through the body.

The correct answer is C:) Inability to sleep while sitting up. In some cases, the person can only sleep while sitting up because of buildup of fluid in the lungs.

109) Chronic means

A) Serious
B) Of long duration
C) Severe
D) Painful

The correct answer is B:) Of the long duration. Chronic refers to a disease of long duration.

110) If you are comatose, the person making the health decisions for you is called your

A) Living will
B) Doctor
C) Surrogate
D) Family

The correct answer is C:) Surrogate. A surrogate is the person who has power of attorney over your health. This exists if you have created a living will giving that person the power. Usually this person is a close family member.

111) Which of the following correctly lists the stages of an infectious disease?

A) Prodromal, Invasive, Incubation, Convalescence
>B) Incubation, Prodromal, Invasive, Convalescence
C) Incubation, Convalescence, Invasive, Prodromal
D) Convalescence, Invasive, Prodromal, Incubation

The correct answer is B:) Incubation, Prodromal, Invasive, Convalescence.

112) What is social death?

> A) When a person, who is still living, is excluded from society.
B) When a person dies in a public place.
C) Learning about death in school while talking to friends.
D) Reading a book in which one of the main characters dies.

The correct answer is A:) When a person, who is still living, is excluded from society.

113) For which of the following is HCG used?

A) To make a person grow taller
B) To help hair grow thicker
> C) To determine if a woman is pregnant
D) To make a person's nails grow faster

The correct answer is C:) To determine if a woman is pregnant.

114) The chickenpox patient is:

> A) Highly contagious two days before the onset of the rash
B) Highly contagious four days before the onset of the rash
C) Highly contagious one week before the onset of the rash
D) Not contagious at all

The correct answer is A:) Highly contagious two days before the onset of the rash.

115) What is the name for an atom with an unpaired electron?

A) Mutated atom
B) Free radical
C) Isotope
D) Off-balance atom

The correct answer is B:) Free radical. An isotope is an atom with an irregular number of neutrons. Answers A and C are not real terms.

116) Categories of chronic diseases include

A) Skin and stomach disorders
B) Pulmonary disorders and motor and facial tics
C) Pain and rectal disorders
D) Motor and vocal tics

The correct answer is A:) Skin and stomach disorders. A is the only completely correct answer. Skin and stomach disorders are included in the list of chronic disorders.

117) Which of the following blood pressures would be considered hypertensive?

A) 130/85
B) 120/80
C) 135/85
D) 150/95

The correct answer is D:) 150/95. Any pressure above 140/90 is considered hypertensive.

118) COPD stands for

A) Chronic Rectal Obstruction Disorder
B) Coordinator of Patient Diseases
C) Chronic Obstructive Pulmonary Disease
D) Certified Obstructive Pediatric

The correct answer is C:) Chronic Obstructive Pulmonary Disease. COPD refers to Chronic Obstructive Pulmonary Disease.

119) COPDs include

A) Bronchitis, emphysema, and asthma
B) Chickenpox, bulimia, and arthritis
C) Crohn's disease, anxiety attacks, and bronchitis
D) Bronchitis, arthritis, and tonsillitis

The correct answer is A:) Bronchitis, emphysema, and asthma. COPDs are lung disorders; thus bronchitis, emphysema, and asthma are the correct answers.

120) Emphysema is

A) Definitely hereditary
B) Not conclusively shown to be hereditary
C) Caused by polluted environments
D) Aggravated by cigarette smoking

The correct answer is D:) Aggravated by cigarette smoking. This is the only answer that can be stated with certainty.

121) Which of the following is NOT a symptom of type II diabetes?

A) Low blood sugar
B) Fatigue
C) Blurred vision
D) Excess thirst

The correct answer is A:) Low blood sugar. Type II diabetes is when the muscle, fat and liver cells don't respond normally to insulin. Because of this glucose cannot be stored in the cells, causing high blood sugar, not low blood sugar.

122) Chronic skin diseases include

A) Eczema, rosacea, skin cancer
B) Measles, rosacea, and skin cancer
C) Poison ivy, ringworm, and eczema
D) Psoriasis, chickenpox, and insect bites

The correct answer is B:) Measles, rosacea, and skin cancer.

123) What is the definition of immunization?

A) When a person is born immune to a disease they are called an "immunized" person.
B) Being immunized by having killed or weakened pathogens introduced into a system.
C) Eliminating a disease from natural occurrence.
D) The process by which a person becomes immune to a disease.

The correct answer is D:) The process by which a person becomes immune to a disease. Answer B is the definition of vaccination, which while it is a type of immunization is not the correct definition.

124) Pressing your hand up against the wall is an example of what kind of exercise?

A) Isotonic
B) Isokinetic
C) Aerobic
D) Anaerobic

The correct answer is A:) Isotonic. Isotonic exercises are where your muscle contracts, but your joints don't move and the muscle fibers stay at the same length.

125) Which of the following is correct?

A) A tic is a pulse-like feeling in the chest
B) A tic is a small flying insect that bites
C) A tic is a repeated, uncontrollable burst of movement or speech
D) A tic may be either a motor tic or a vocal tic

The correct answer is C:) A tic is a repeated, uncontrollable burst of movement or speech. A tic is an involuntary movement or utterance.

126) What does HCG stand for?

A) Human Chorionic Gonadotrophin
B) Human Calcitic Gonadotrophin
C) Human Chorionic Gonaphin
D) Human Chorionic Glucocorticoid

The correct answer is A:) Human Chorionic Gonadotrophin.

127) Chronic pain is

A) A continuing pain over a long period of time
B) A sudden pain that has a beginning and an end
C) Untreatable
D) A possible cause of appendicitis

The correct answer is A:) A continuing pain over a long period of time.

128) Which of the following is true?

A) Eustress is a negative form a stress.
B) Eustress is a positive form of stress.
C) Distress is a positive form of stress.
D) Eustress and distress are both positive forms of stress.

The correct answer is B:) Eustress is a positive form of stress. Eustress is controlled and productive. It's the "good" kind of stress.

129) Fibromyalgia is

A) The second most common form of rheumatism
B) Similar to arthritis in that it affects the bones and joints of the body
C) Dissimilar to arthritis because it affects the ligaments and muscles of the body
D) A mental disorder

The correct answer is C:) Dissimilar to arthritis because it affects the ligaments and muscles of the body. Unlike arthritis, fibromyalgia strikes the muscles and ligaments of the body.

130) Which of the following statements is true?

A) Fibromyalgia may worsen in warm climates
B) Fibromyalgia improves with physical exertion
C) Fibromyalgia strikes more males than females
D) Fibromyalgia affects almost 4 million Americans

The correct answer is D:) Fibromyalgia affects almost 4 million Americans. Fibromyalgia is prevalent in our society, affecting 3.7 million Americans.

131) Autoimmune diseases are:

A) The second most prevalent in our society
B) Caused by some immune antigens attacking themselves
C) Are generally contagious
D) Are not subject to hormonal and environmental influences

The correct answer is B:) Caused by some immune antigens attacking themselves. Autoimmune diseases result from antigens attacking themselves or other healthy antigens.

132) Which of the following effects does trans-fat have?

A) Heighten LDL, Lower HDL
B) Heighten HDL, Lower LDL
C) Heighten both LDL and HDL
D) Lower both LDL and HDL

The correct answer is A:) Heighten LDL, Lower HDL. For this reason, trans-fat is considered very unhealthy.

133) Sjogren's disease

A) Affects 3 million Americans
B) Affects men more than women
C) Is generally not thought to be a genetic disorder
D) Is caused by an inflammation of the glands

The correct answer is D:) Is caused by an inflammation of the glands.

134) Sjogren's disease is:

A) Found less often in families where other family members have developed an autoimmune disease
B) Caused by an identifiable substance
C) Characterized by extreme dryness in the affected glands
D) Curable but only over a long period of time

The correct answer is C:) Characterized by extreme dryness in the affected glands. Sjogren's patients experience extreme dryness, particularly in the eyes and mouth.

135) What is mitral valve prolapse?

A) When the mitral valve closes off for longer than it should.
B) When the mitral valve gets clogged.
C) When the mitral valve doesn't close properly.
D) When the mitral valve stays closed, stopping the flow of blood.

The correct answer is C:) When the mitral valve doesn't close properly. The heart is designed so that blood flows in one direction. When the mitral valve doesn't close it, allows blood to flow "backwards" when the heart contracts.

136) Cancer is:

A) The result of healthy cells living too long; they just "hang out" in the body
B) The grouping together of cancer cells, forming a tumor
C) Highly contagious
D) Tumors spontaneously develop in different areas of the body, known as "spreading."

The correct answer is B:) The grouping together of cancer cells, forming a tumor.

137) Mouth cancer is:

A) An oral cavity cancer
B) Possibly, but not likely, caused by tobacco usage and excessive alcohol consumption
C) Caused by poor dental care
D) Caused by a virus

The correct answer is A:) An oral cavity cancer. Mouth cancer is one type of oral cavity cancer.

138) HMOs are:

A) The same as traditional insurance companies
B) Less reliable than traditional insurance companies
C) More costly than traditional insurance companies
D) Not accepted by many doctors

The correct answer is D:) Not accepted by many doctors.

139) If you experience difficulty with an insurance matter, you should:

A) Hire a lawyer
B) Refuse to pay any amount
C) Appeal to your state Insurance Commission
D) Expect your doctor to work out a solution with your insurance company

The correct answer is C:) Appeal to your state Insurance Commission. Starting the appeals process is the starting point for your solution.

140) After studying the risks factors for several diseases, what one risk factor is listed for almost every disease?

A) Stress
B) Smoking cigarettes
C) Dietary deficiencies
D) Rapid, repetitive changes in weight

The correct answer is B:) Smoking cigarettes. While each of these items is a risk factor for several diseases, the one factor that is repeated for every disease studied is smoking cigarettes.

141) Which disease has been eliminated thanks to the development and distribution of its vaccine?

A) Measles
B) Smallpox
C) Chickenpox
D) Mumps

The correct answer is B:) Smallpox.

142) Which is NOT a risk factors for pancreatic cancer?

A) Too much sodium in diet
B) Cigarette smoking, alcohol, and a diet high in butter fat or meats
C) Family history
D) Obesity

The correct answer is A:) Too much sodium in diet. Answer choices B, C, and D are all risk factors for pancreatic cancer.

143) Which of the following theory used for evaluation is based on biology?

A) Biological
B) Cognitive
C) Humanistic
D) Psychoanalytical

The correct answer is A:) Biological. This theory used for evaluation is based on biology.

144) To evaluate a person using this approach, one must study and observe behavior

A) Biological
B) Behavioral
C) Humanistic
D) Psychoanalytical

The correct answer is B:) Behavioral. To evaluate a person using this approach, one must study and observe behavior.

145) __________ theorists examine how the mind is involved in learning.

A) Biological
B) Cognitive
C) Humanistic
D) Psychoanalytical

The correct answer is B:) Cognitive. Cognitive theorists examine how the mind is involved in knowing, learning, remembering and thinking. They study how the mind relates to behavior.

146) Which of the following describes vasocongestion?

A) The heart doesn't circulate a sufficient amount of blood through the system.
B) When a person's blood vessels don't close off, and blood begins to flow backwards.
C) Increased blood flow to an area of the body causes increased in blood pressure and swelling of tissue.
D) When the mitral valve stays closed, stopping the flow of blood.

The correct answer is C:) Increased blood flow to an area of the body causes increased in blood pressure and swelling of tissue. Answer A describes congestive heart failure. Answers B and D describe mitral valve prolapse.

147) Which of the following types of Medicare covers hospital stays?

A) Part A
B) Part B
C) Part C
D) Part D

The correct answer is A:) Part A. Medicare Part A (Hospital Insurance) helps cover inpatient care in hospitals. Part A also helps cover skilled nursing facility, hospice, and home health care if you meet certain conditions.

148) Which of the following statements does NOT support the Wear and Tear Theory of Aging?

A) The body has an infinite capacity to repair damage.
B) Alcoholics often die from liver failure.
C) People can die in car crashes.
D) People who smoke cigarettes tend to have shortened lifespans.

The correct answer is A:) The body has an infinite capacity to repair damage. This statement directly contradicts the Wear and Tear Theory because if the body had an infinite capacity to repair damage, then it wouldn't get worn out.

149) The most important risk factor for bladder cancer is

A) Cigarette smoking
B) Obesity
C) Long-term use of over-the-counter drugs
D) Cigar smoking

The correct answer is A:) Cigarette smoking. The highest risk factor for bladder cancer is cigarette smoking.

150) Which of the following is NOT a responsibility of the EPA?

A) Communications
B) Protection of endangered species
C) Hazardous waste
D) Drinking water quality

The correct answer is A:) Communications. Answers A, B, and C are all responsibilities of the EPA.

151) Risk factors for leukemia include:

A) Family history
B) High doses of ionizing radiation
C) Pesticides
D) All of the above

The correct answer is D:) All of the above.

152) In which stage of death would a person most likely say "There must be a mistake?"

A) Bargaining
B) Depression
C) Acceptance
D) Denial

The correct answer is D:) Denial.

153) Women may lessen the risks of developing cancer by

A) Having regular examinations by the family doctor
B) Having regular Pap smears
C) Practicing breast self-examination
D) All of the above

The correct answer is D:) All of the above. All of the above are steps that may lessen the risk of cancer in women.

154) The four general treatments for cancer are

A) Chemotherapy, radiation, surgery, and drugs
B) Chemotherapy, surgery, acupuncture, and drugs
C) Surgery, herbals, drugs, and chemotherapy
D) Herbals, natural drugs, and surgery

The correct answer is A:) Chemotherapy, radiation, surgery, and drugs. While treatments vary greatly among patients, Answer A represents the common treatment types.

155) Rheumatoid arthritis is described as systemic, which means

A) It is concentrated in one body system
B) It starts as a single illness, but gradually affects the whole body
C) In addition to joint inflammation, it can spread to other organs of the body
D) It can start anywhere in the body, but it moves systematically (in a pattern) through the entire body

The correct answer is C:) In addition to joint inflammation, it can spread to other organs of the body. Systemic means it can attack other organs of the body.

156) Which of the following is NOT characteristic of hospice?

A) Involving a patient and their family in the patient's care.
B) Controlling the symptoms of the patient's illness as much as possible.
C) Round the clock care overseen by a qualified physician.
D) Forcing the patient to care for themselves increases their sense of independence.

The correct answer is D:) Forcing the patient to care for themselves increases their sense of independence. While the hospice system is designed to increase the patient's feeling of control, it is not done by forcing them to care for themselves.

157) Rheumatoid arthritis affects

A) The joints
B) The muscles
C) The face
D) The liver

The correct answer is A:) The joints. Rheumatoid arthritis is a painful disease of the joints.

158) Rheumatoid arthritis...

A) May go into remission and then return in its same severity
B) Never goes into remission; there is no treatment for it
C) Causes painful inflammation of the left leg only
D) Given time, it spreads to the muscles

The correct answer is A:) May go into remission and then return in its same severity.

159) Do all cancers spread?

A) Yes, because both benign and malignant tumors are capable of spreading to surrounding tissue.
B) Yes, because malignant tumors spread through surrounding tissue and organs.
C) No, because neither benign nor malignant tumors are capable of spreading to surrounding tissue.
D) No, because only benign tumors can spread.

The correct answer is D:) No, because only benign tumors can spread. Malignant tumors spread by attacking the cells in nearby tissue and organs. Benign tumors remain localized. While Answer B is a correct statement, it is an incorrect response to the question.

160) Which one of the following statements is TRUE?

A) Cigarette smoking is definitely a high risk factor for developing heart disease
B) Cigar and pipe smoking are low risk factors for developing heart disease
C) Secondhand smoke is not a risk factor for developing heart disease
D) Chewing tobacco is not a risk for heart disease

The correct answer is A:) Cigarette smoking is definitely a high risk factor for developing heart disease. Cigarette smoking is a serious risk for developing heart disease.

161) Diabetes is

A) The failure of the body to produce or properly use insulin
B) Is either Type 1 or Type 2
C) Caused by an unknown environmental factor triggers the onset of diabetes.
D) All of the above

The correct answer is D:) All of the above.

162) Is there a link between exercise and memory?

A) Yes, because recent studies show that regular exercise increases neuron production.
B) Yes, because recent studies show that regular exercise decreases neuron production.
C) No, because people are born with a set number of neurons.
D) No, because recent studies show that regular exercise increases neuron production.

The correct answer is A:) Yes, because recent studies show that regular exercise increases neuron production. Although it was once believed that Answer C was correct, recent studies indicate that it is not. Answer D is a correct statement, but an incorrect answer.

163) Which of the following is NOT true about arthritis?

A) Not connected to genes
B) An autoimmune disease
C) Possibly curable
D) Currently incurable

The correct answer is A:) Not connected to genes. The answer choices B, C, and D are true facts about arthritis.

164) Which of the following is NOT something that a person should do in a fire?

A) Run around madly trying to find a way out.
B) Call for help as best as possible.
C) Stay low because smoke rises and there is cleaner air down low.
D) Look for smoke coming from around doors before opening them.

The correct answer is A:) Run around madly trying to find a way out. It's important to be aware of your surroundings, and not just randomly and frantically looking for a way out.

165) Which of the following is TRUE about arthritis?

A) A genetic-related disorder
B) Results from an unknown cause
C) The painful inflammation of the joints
D) All of the above

The correct answer is D:) All of the above.

166) Genetics is

A) The study of genes and how they function in our bodies
B) Such a difficult field that little research is done
C) The subject of much research
D) Researchers are uncovering some exciting, hopeful information is being reported

The correct answer is A:) The study of genes and how they function in our bodies.

167) Gene mutation is

A) A tumor
B) A change
C) Restructuring
D) A disease-producing gene

The correct answer is B:) A change.

168) In which of the following is the systolic pressure 120?

A) 240/2
B) 30/40
C) 120/80
D) 80/120

The correct answer is C:) 120/80. The systolic pressure is represented by the first number, and indicates the pressure during a heartbeat.

169) Which sections of the brain are affected by Alzheimer's disease?

A) Personality, hand/eye coordination, and memory
B) Memory, breathing, and speech
C) Memory, speech, and personality
D) Speech, personality, and breathing

The correct answer is C:) Memory, speech, and personality. Although all of the other answers identify two of the areas correctly, only Answer C correctly identifies all three.

170) Which of the following is NOT true about arthritis?

A) Arthritis is definitely related to genes
B) Which gene is related to arthritis is known
C) Which gene is related to the development of arthritis is unknown
D) Finding the arthritis gene may enable researchers to find a cure

The correct answer is B:) Which gene is related to arthritis is known. The answer choices A, C, and D are true. Arthritis is definitely genetic.

171) Which of the following is NOT a common symptom of Schizophrenia?

A) Heart failure
B) Disorganized thinking patterns
C) Severe hallucinations
D) Lack of emotion

The correct answer is A:) Heart failure. Schizophrenia is a mental disease, not a heart problem.

172) Are all diabetes sufferers' insulin dependent?

A) Yes, because diabetes is always uncontrollable.
B) Yes, because people with type I diabetes cannot produce insulin.
C) No, often people with type II diabetes can control their symptoms though healthy diet and exercise.
D) No, because people with type II diabetes cannot produce insulin.

The correct answer is C:) No, often people with type II diabetes can control their symptoms through healthy diet and exercise. Answer D is incorrect because it is people with type I diabetes who cannot produce insulin. Type II diabetes is when a person's cells do not respond normally to insulin.

173) The study of automobile safety is included in studies about health because

A) An automobile accident frequently results in the need for medical treatment
B) It is the cause of a large number of deaths and long-term injuries
C) The driver's medical condition is often a factor in accidents
D) All of the above

The correct answer is D:) All of the above.

174) You need to drink a minimum of __________ ounces of water a day.

A) 8
B) 32
C) 64
D) 80

The correct answer is C:) 64. You should drink a minimum of 64 ounces of water in a day. This keeps your body hydrated, cool and can even help you lose weight.

175) Which of the following is NOT an example of distracted driving?

A) Talking on a cell phone while driving
B) Listening to distracting and loud music while driving
C) Eating food while driving
D) Driving late at night or early in the morning

The correct answer is D:) Driving late at night or early in the morning. Phones, music, and food are all examples of common distractions in a car.

176) Which of the following describes the Theory of Programmed Aging?

A) There is no specific explanation which describes why an organism dies.
B) Free radicals in the body damage cells and cause death.
C) People are programmed to age and die at a certain time.
D) Lifestyle determines lifespan.

The correct answer is C:) People are programmed to age and die at a certain time. Answer B describes the Free Radical Theory or Aging. Answer D describes the Wear and Tear Theory of Aging.

177) Which of the following is NOT caused by a pathogen?

A) Tuberculosis
B) E. coli
C) Chickenpox
D) Cancer

The correct answer is D:) Cancer. Cancer is a problem within the body's cells, not the result of a pathogen.

178) Automobile safety is:

A) A good starting point because we all either drive or ride in an automobile
B) Out of our control if we are not drivers
C) For someone else. I'm a good driver!
D) Up to the individual driver

The correct answer is A:) A good starting point because we all either driver or ride in an automobile. Automobile safety affects all of us.

179) In what place are cremations usually done?

A) A crematorium
B) A mortuary
C) A funeral home
D) The person's house

The correct answer is A:) A crematorium. As the name indicates, a person is generally cremated in a crematorium.

180) What is an antibody?

A) Cells in the blood stream which help strengthen the veins.
B) Anything which triggers a response from the immune system.
C) A substance produced by B cells to help protect the body from infection.
D) A cell which mistakenly attacks the cells in a person's own body.

The correct answer is C:) A substance produced by B cells to help protect the body from infection. Answer B refers to antigens.

181) Which of the following is NOT an example of social death?

A) When a dying person is referred to as if they were already dead.
B) When a person in a play acts out the part of a dying character.
C) When a dying person is excluded from conversations.
D) When a dying person is moved to a terminal ward and given little care.

The correct answer is B:) When a person in a play acts out the part of a dying character.

182) The __________ phase happens when you are exposed to a stressor.

A) Alarm
B) Resistance
C) Exhaustion
D) None of the above

The correct answer is A:) Alarm. The alarm phase happens when you are exposed to a stressor.

183) What is hospice?

A) A system of care in which the family is excluded from the treatment of the patient.
B) A system of care designed to treat people with severe illnesses.
C) A system of care for terminally ill people which is not designed to treat illness, but to make the dying process as comfortable as possible.
D) A system of care designed to test innovative treatments for supposedly incurable diseases.

The correct answer is C:) A system of care for terminally ill people which is not designed to treat illness, but to make the dying process as comfortable as possible. Answers A, B and D all refer to treatment, which is not the purpose of hospice programs.

184) The process of the body returning to normal and maintaining itself is called returning to __________ .

A) Homeostasis
B) Exhaustion
C) Alarm
D) GAS

The correct answer is A:) Homeostasis. Homeostasis is what it is called when the body maintains the status quo.

185) When the extra energy created by the body is depleted it is called

A) Alarm phase
B) Resistance phase
C) Exhaustion phase
D) None of the above

The correct answer is C:) Exhaustion phase. When the extra energy is depleted from the body it is called the exhaustion phase.

186) A person who now gives up in the face of a challenge or difficulty consistently because they have failed in the past is showing

A) Learned helplessness
B) Quitter syndrome
C) Prejudice
D) None of the above

The correct answer is A:) Learned helplessness. A person who now gives up in the face of a challenge or difficulty consistently because they have failed in the past is showing learned helplessness.

187) Is it possible for a person to increase their alcohol tolerance?

A) Yes, because the kidneys adapt by filtering alcohol out of the blood faster.
B) No, because the body isn't capable of adapting.
C) Yes, because the liver adapts by producing more of the necessary enzymes.
D) No, because it isn't possible for the liver to produce more enzymes than it already does.

The correct answer is C:) Yes, because the liver adapts by producing more of the necessary enzymes. It is the liver that metabolizes the alcohol, not the kidney filtering it out.

188) A large percentage of automobile accidents happen because:

A) The driver is under the influence of alcohol or drugs
B) The driver is distracted, both by outside and inside happenings
C) The driver fails to look out for a careless driver in his traffic setting
D) All of the above

The correct answer is D:) All of the above. All of these answers can contribute or be the cause of an automobile accident.

189) Which of the following is TRUE?

A) Medicare is only available to low-income families.
B) Medicaid are enjoyed by nearly 40 million Americans.
C) Individual insurance policies (as opposed to group policies) are very expensive.
D) You cannot sue an insurance company if you have been denied rights.

The correct answer is C:) Individual insurance policies (as opposed to group policies) are very expensive. Perhaps you confused Medicare and Medicaid in the answer selections.

190) What is the term for the main cause of acute alcohol intoxication?

A) If a person's liver doesn't metabolize alcohol properly
B) Alcohol poisoning
C) Overdrinking
D) Binge drinking

The correct answer is D:) Binge drinking. Alcohol poisoning (Answer B) is another name for acute alcohol intoxication, not the cause. Overdrinking (Answer C) is technically the cause of acute alcohol intoxication, however it is a description for binge drinking, and the question is "What is the term…"

191) HMO stands for

A) Home Management Organizations
B) Health Management Offices
C) Health Management Organizations
D) Health/Medical Options

The correct answer is C:) Health Management Organizations.

192) Which of the following is NOT a symptom of diabetes?

A) Feeling full of energy
B) Blurry vision
C) Weight gain
D) Excessive thirst

The correct answer is A:) Feeling full of energy. Fatigue is a symptom of diabetes, as are blurry vision, weight gain, and excessive thirst.

193) Employer health plans:

A) May require a partial premium payment by the employee.
B) Employer health plans never require a partial payment by the employee; they are part of the "perks."
C) Employer health plans never follow an employee into retirement.
D) Employees should shop other plans before enrolling in the employer's plan. You may pay less for another plan.

The correct answer is A:) May require a partial premium payment by the employee. Individual coverage is never less expensive than employer group plans.

194) Approximately what amount of women require a blood transfusion due to excessive bleeding?

A) 1/10
B) 1/100
C) 1/1,000
D) 1/10,000

The correct answer is C:) 1/1,000.

195) You have a neonate. This means you have a

A) Chronic disease
B) Bacteria
C) Infection
D) Newborn

The correct answer is D:) Newborn. A neonate is another word for a newborn baby.

196) Chickenpox is also known as

A) Vaccination
B) Variety of diseases
C) Varicella
D) Small pox

The correct answer is C:) Varicella. The scientific name for chickenpox is varicella.

197) Antibiotics are not effective with diseases caused by

A) Virus
B) Bacteria
C) Contagion
D) Germs

The correct answer is A:) Virus. Antibiotics are not effective with diseases caused by a virus.

198) Chickenpox typically leaves

A) No scars
B) Some scars
C) Large scars
D) Dark scars

The correct answer is B:) Some scars. Chickenpox often leaves some light scars.

199) What does HIV stand for?

A) Human Insufficiency Virus
B) Helper Insufficiency Virus
C) Helper Immunodeficiency Virus
D) Human Immunodeficiency Virus

The correct answer is D:) Human Immunodeficiency Virus.

200) Shingles

A) Is a chickenpox-like disease
B) May recur several times after the initial bout
C) Is a disease that appears in adults who have never had chickenpox
D) Usually occurs all over the body

The correct answer is A:) Is a chickenpox-like disease. Shingles is a chickenpox-like disease from the virus varicella.

201) Accident prevention is:

A) A critical study, directly affecting our lives
B) Difficult because we can't control the other person
C) Good for school kids but not as important in adult lives
D) Limited in its effectiveness

The correct answer is A:) A critical study, directly affecting our lives. Accident prevention is a critical study.

202) Which of the following is NOT true of pathogens?

A) Pathogens are organisms which cause disease.
B) Pathogens are capable of spreading through food, air, and contact.
C) Bacteria and fungus are the only types of pathogens.
D) Tuberculosis, Measles, and Athlete's Foot are all caused by pathogens.

The correct answer is C:) Bacteria and fungus are the only types of pathogens. Pathogens can come from many sources other than bacteria and fungus, such as virus.

203) __________ theory revolves around the individual's unconscious motivation.

A) Biological
B) Cognitive
C) Humanistic
D) Psychoanalytical

The correct answer is D:) Psychoanalytical. The psychoanalytical theory revolves around the individual's unconscious motivation.

204) Which is the fourth stage of Maslow's Hierarchy of Needs?

A) Self-actualization
B) Esteem needs
C) Belonging and love
D) Safety

The correct answer is B:) Esteem needs.

205) Allergens are

A) Substances that stop an allergic reaction
B) Substances that cause allergic reactions
C) Substances that carry allergies
D) Substances that must be isolated

The correct answer is B:) Substances that cause allergic reactions. Allergens are substances that cause the manifestation of an allergy.

206) Chronic typically describes a condition:

A) For which there is treatment but no cure
B) For which there is both a treatment and a cure
C) For which there is neither a treatment nor a cure
D) Which is serious and usually fatal

The correct answer is A:) For which there is treatment but no cure. It is usually applied to diseases which can be treated but not cured.

207) Which of the following types of Medicare covers prescription drugs?

A) Part A
B) Part B
C) Part C
D) Part D

The correct answer is D:) Part D. Medicare Part D covers prescription drugs.

208) Which is the second stage of Maslow's Hierarchy of Needs?

A) Self-actualization
B) Esteem needs
C) Belonging and love
D) Safety

The correct answer is D:) Safety.

209) A fertilized ovum or egg is referred to as

A) Neonate
B) Zygote
C) Anoxia
D) Uterus

The correct answer is B:) Zygote.

210) A mother first feels her baby kick at around

A) 1 week
B) 4 weeks
C) 13 weeks
D) 40 weeks

The correct answer is C:) 13 weeks. The first feelings of movement from a fetus can be felt by the mother from between 13 weeks and 25 weeks. These first movements can be referred to as "quickening." Even though a fetus begins movement as early as five weeks, the range the mother feels her baby move is somewhat larger.

211) The gradual increase of the earth's temperature is due to?

A) Green Revolution
B) Greenhouse effect
C) Acid rain
D) Overpopulation

The correct answer is B:) Greenhouse effect. The greenhouse effect, also known as global warming, relates to the gradual warming of the earth's temperature.

212) Which of the following is a true statement?

A) LDL stands for Low Density Lipoproteins and is considered "good cholesterol"
B) LDL and HDL are both considered "good cholesterol"
C) HDL stands for High Density Lipoproteins and is considered "good cholesterol"
D) LDL and HDL are both considered "bad cholesterol"

The correct answer is C:) HDL stands for High Density Lipoproteins and is considered "good cholesterol." On the other hand, LDL stands for Low Density Lipoproteins and is considered "bad cholesterol."

213) Patients with mumps should be given

A) Lots of fruit juices because of the nutritional value
B) No fruit juices because of the acidic content
C) A regular diet
D) No special diet

The correct answer is B:) No fruit juices because of the acidic content. The acidity of fruit juices may irritate the already sore throat.

214) What does BMR stand for?

A) Base Metabolic Rate
B) Basal Metabolic Rate
C) Base Movement Rate
D) Basal Movement Rate

The correct answer is B:) Basal Metabolic Rate. This is the amount of energy expended while at rest.

215) Mouth sores appear in some measles patients. These sores are known as:

A) Dr. Freud's sores
B) Madam Curie's sores
C) Dr. Koplik's sores
D) Dr. Livingston's sores

The correct answer is C:) Dr. Koplik's sores. The sores are named for named for Henry Koplik, an American pediatrician.

216) What cancer is HPV believed to cause?

A) Breast cancer
B) Colon cancer
C) Cervical cancer
D) Brain cancer

The correct answer is C:) Cervical cancer.

217) The portion that you must pay first before your insurance company pays a percentage of your medical costs

A) Yearly limits
B) Deductible
C) Out of pocket
D) Monthly premium

The correct answer is B:) Deductible. While you do need to pay your monthly premium to keep current on your insurance, the most correct answer is deductible.

Test-Taking Strategies

Here are some test-taking strategies that are specific to this test and to other DSST tests in general:

- Keep your eyes on the time. Pay attention to how much time you have left.
- Read the entire question and read all the answers. Many questions are not as hard to answer as they may seem. Sometimes, a difficult sounding question really only is asking you how to read an accompanying chart. Chart and graph questions are on most DANTES/DSST tests and should be an easy free point.
- If you don't know the answer immediately, the new computer-based testing lets you mark questions and come back to them later if you have time.
- Read the wording carefully. Some words can give you hints to the right answer. There are no exceptions to an answer when there are words in the question such as always, all or none. If one of the answer choices includes most or some of the right answers, but not all, then that is not the answer. Here is an example:

The primary colors include all of the following:

A) Red, Yellow, Blue, Green

B) Red, Green, Yellow

C) Red, Orange, Yellow

D) Red, Yellow, Blue

Although item A includes all the right answers, it also includes an incorrect answer, making it incorrect. If you didn't read it carefully, was in a hurry, or didn't know the material well, you might fall for this.

- Make a guess on a question that you do not know the answer to. There is no penalty for an incorrect answer. Eliminate the answer choices that you know are incorrect. For example, this will let your guess be a 1 in 3 chance instead.

Test Preparation

How much you need to study depends on your knowledge of a subject area. If you are interested in literature, took it in school, or enjoy reading then your study and preparation for the literature or humanities test will not need to be as intensive as that of someone who is new to literature.

This book is much different than the regular DANTES study guides. This book actually teaches you the information that you need to know to pass the test. If you are particularly interested in an area, or feel that you want more information, do a quick search online. We've tried not to include too much depth in areas that are not as essential on the test. Everything in this book will be on the test. It is important to understand all major theories and concepts listed in the table of contents. It is also important to know any bolded words.

Don't worry if you do not understand or know a lot about the area. With minimal study, you can complete and pass the test.

Legal Note

FLASHCARDS

This section contains flashcards for you to use to further your understanding of the material and test yourself on important concepts, names or dates. Read the term or question then flip the page over to check the answer on the back. Keep in mind that this information may not be covered in the text of the study guide. Take your time to study the flashcards, you will need to know and understand these concepts to pass the test.

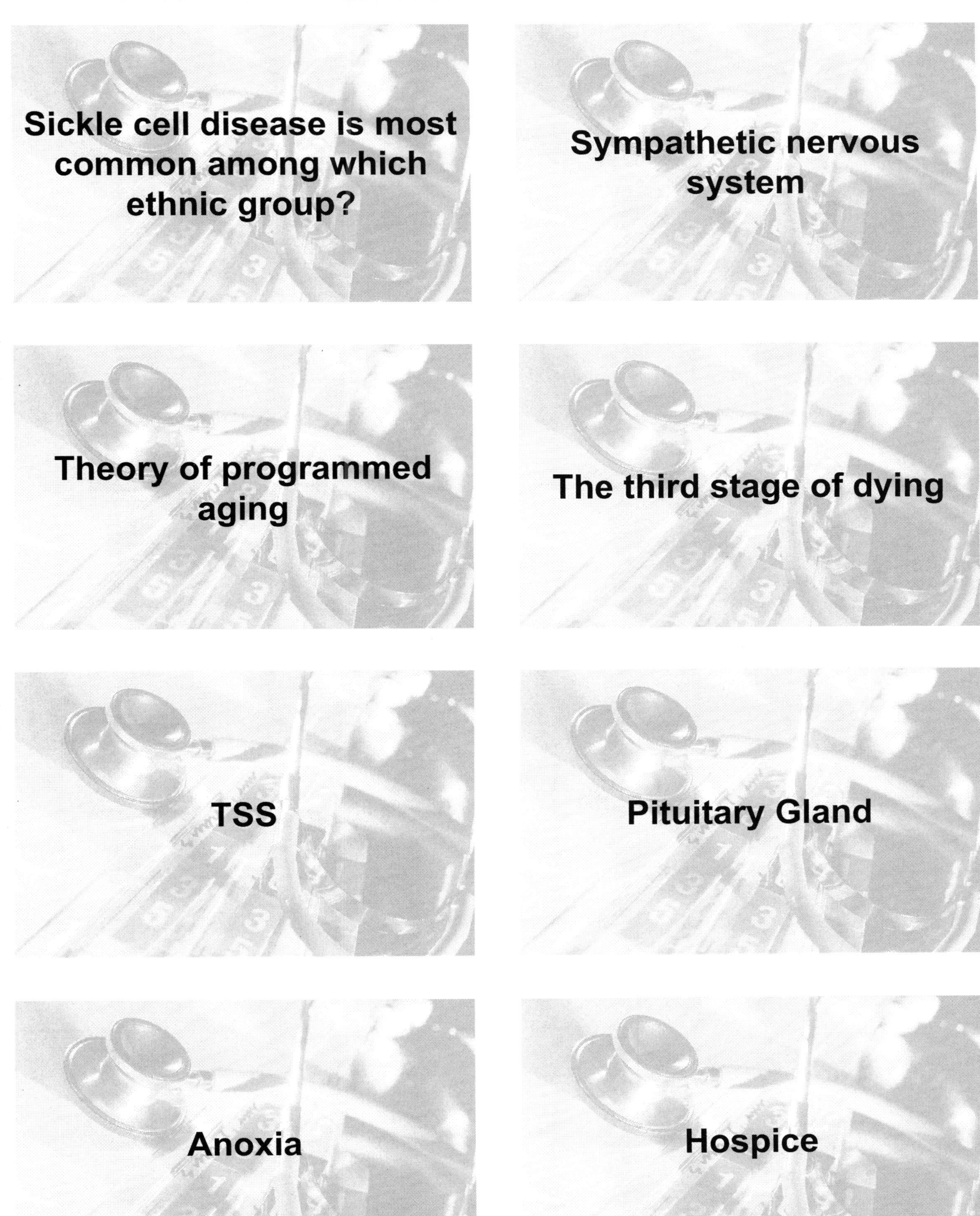
Sickle cell disease is most common among which ethnic group?
Sympathetic nervous system
Theory of programmed aging
The third stage of dying
TSS
Pituitary Gland
Anoxia
Hospice

Arousing part of the nervous system

African Americans

Bargaining

Idea that death is a programmed into the body

Gland that controls hormones

Toxic Shock Syndrome

A system of care for terminally or incurably ill

Brain damage caused by failing to breathe

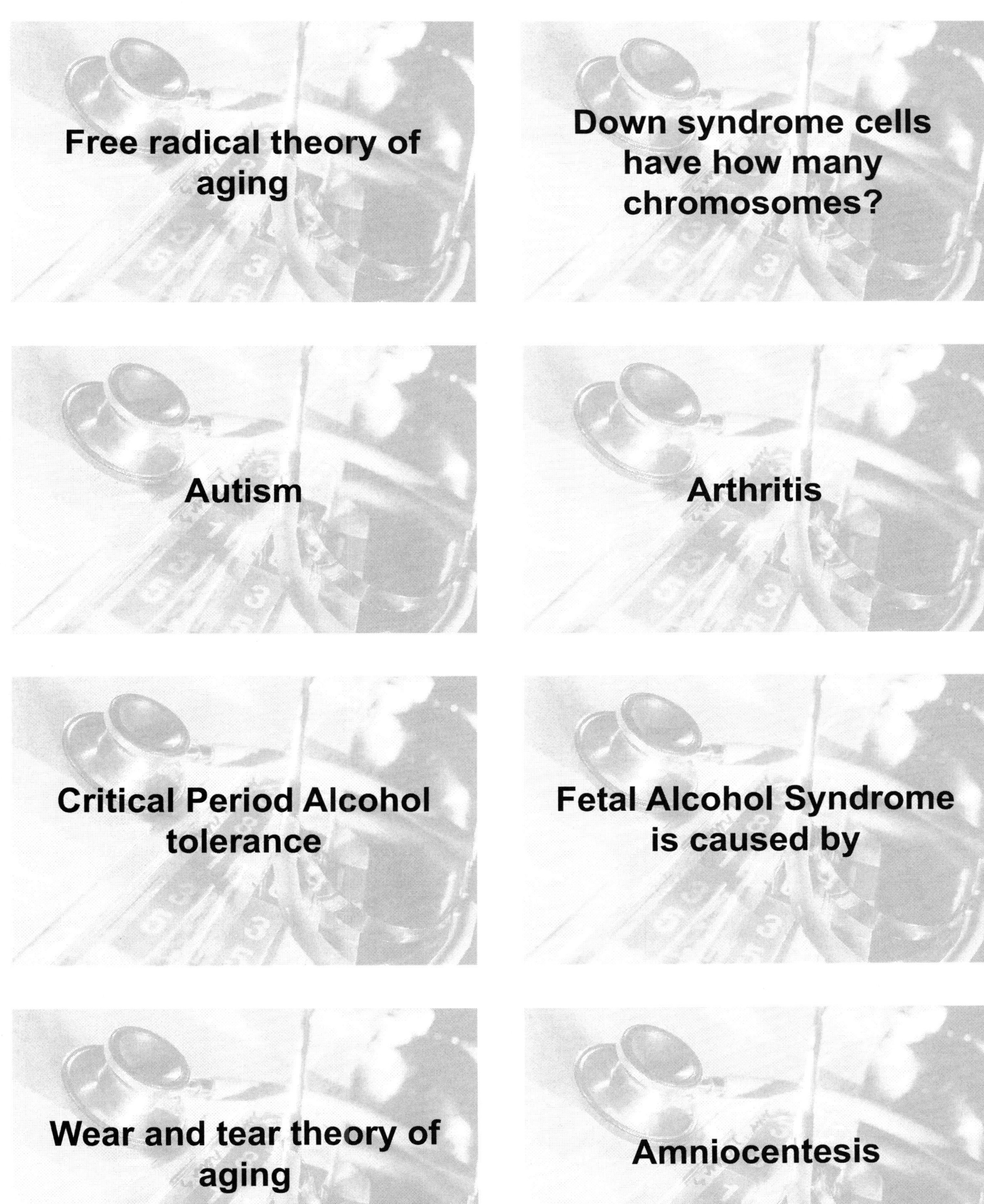
Free radical theory of aging
Down syndrome cells have how many chromosomes?
Autism
Arthritis
Critical Period Alcohol tolerance
Fetal Alcohol Syndrome is caused by
Wear and tear theory of aging
Amniocentesis

47

The body continuously produces free radicals, which causes a continuous stream of damage

A disease in the joints which causes inflammation

Lack of responsiveness to other people

Mother's drinking alcohol while pregnant

The rate at which a person's liver can metabolize alcohol

Sample of amniotic sac to be tested for various diseases

The belief that as time goes on damage to the body accumulates

Anorexia Nervosa
Cremation
Acute alcohol intoxication
SIDS
Nature vs. Nurture
Wear-and-Tear Theory
Autoimmune Theory
Alzheimer's Disease

Burning dead person's remains

Self-starvation

Sudden Infant Death Syndrome

Alcohol poisoning

The human body wears out

Are personalities determined by biology or environment?

A chronic condition that deteriorates the nerve fibers in the brain

As our bodies age, our immune systems become less effective

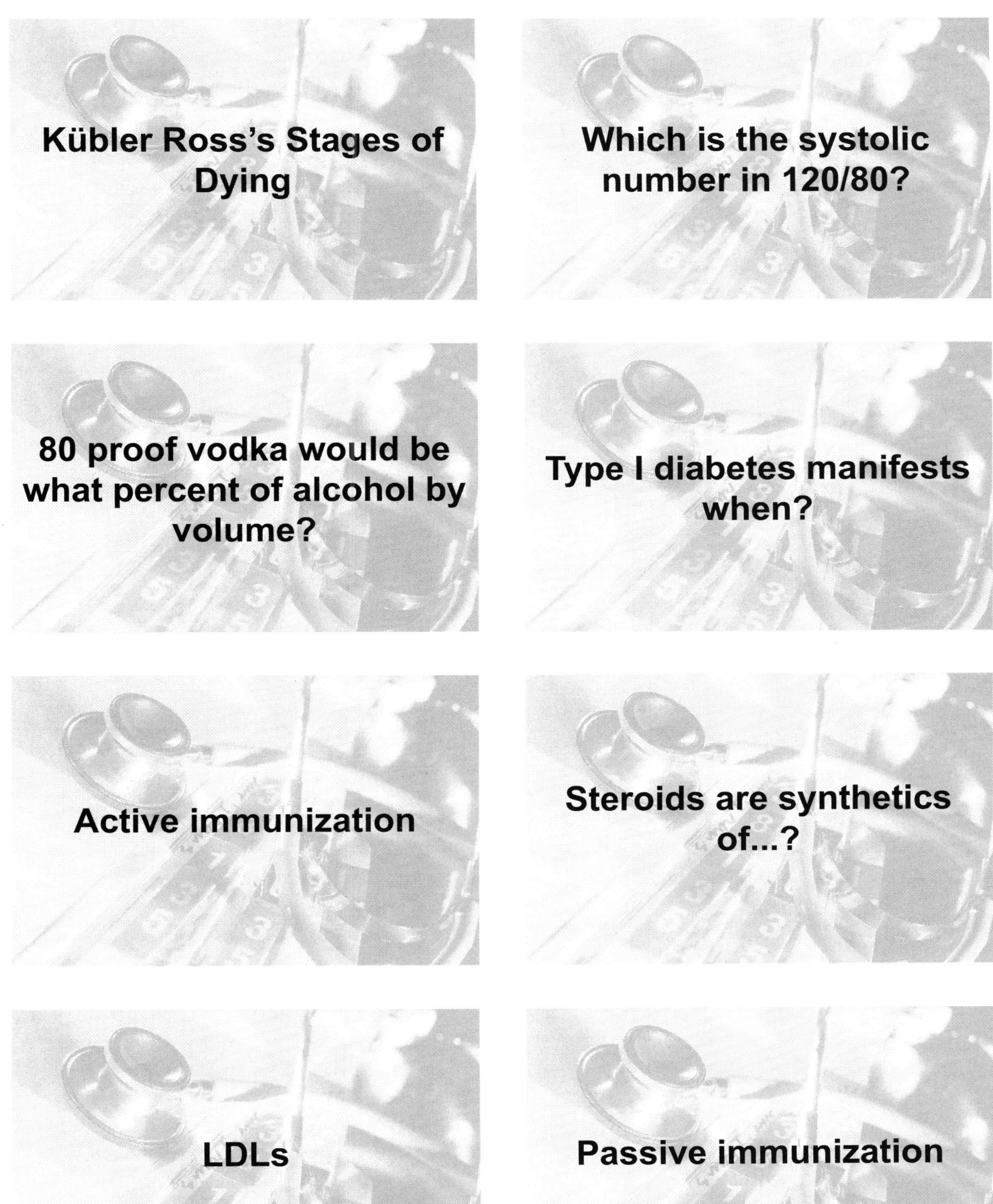
Kübler Ross's Stages of Dying
Which is the systolic number in 120/80?
80 proof vodka would be what percent of alcohol by volume?
Type I diabetes manifests when?
Active immunization
Steroids are synthetics of...?
LDLs
Passive immunization

The first number, 120

1. Denial, 2. Anger,
3. Bargaining,
4. Preparatory Depression,
5. Acceptance

Early in life

40%

Testosterone

When the antigen is directly introduced into a system

Transferring already made antibodies to another person

Bad cholesterol

Epidemic
Overload Principle
Isometric
Concentric
Pathogen
Hypertrophy
How many daily servings of breads, cereals, rice and pasta group?
How many daily servings of the vegetable group?

Beginning by setting a base level for your strength then overloading your muscle

When a disease spreads far above the expected infection rate for a specific group of people in a specific place

Force produced while the muscle is shortening

Force produced without any joint movement

Increased size (girth) of a muscle

Organism which causes disease

3-5 servings

6-11 servings

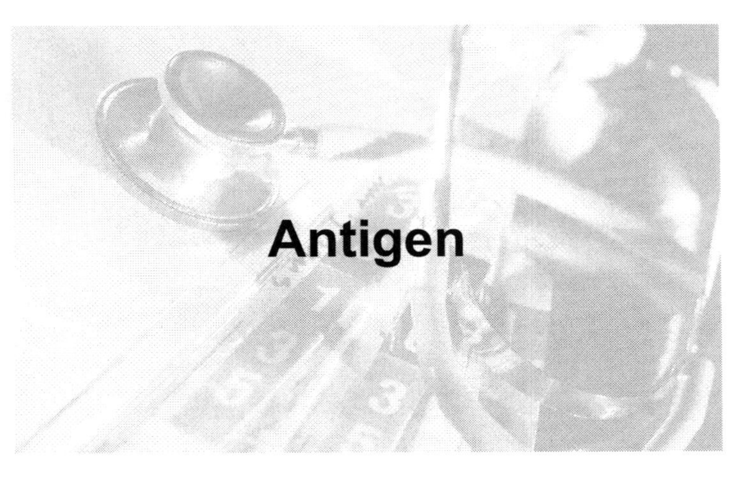
Antigen

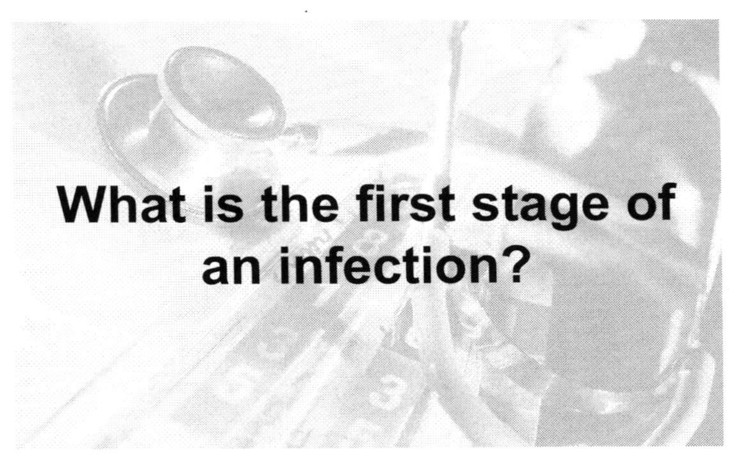
What is the first stage of an infection?

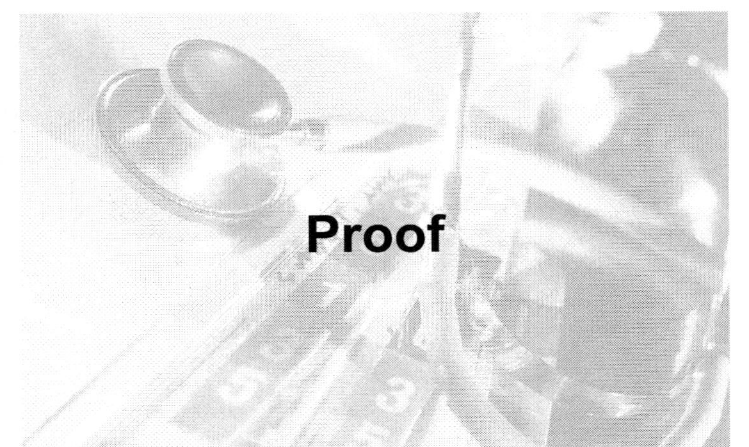
Proof

HCG

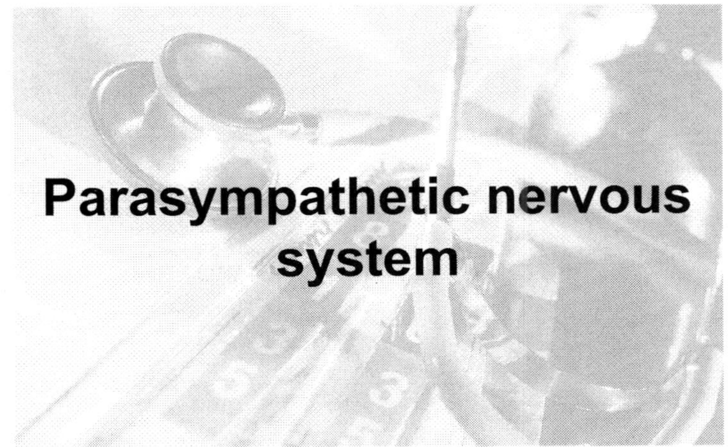
Parasympathetic nervous system

Neonate

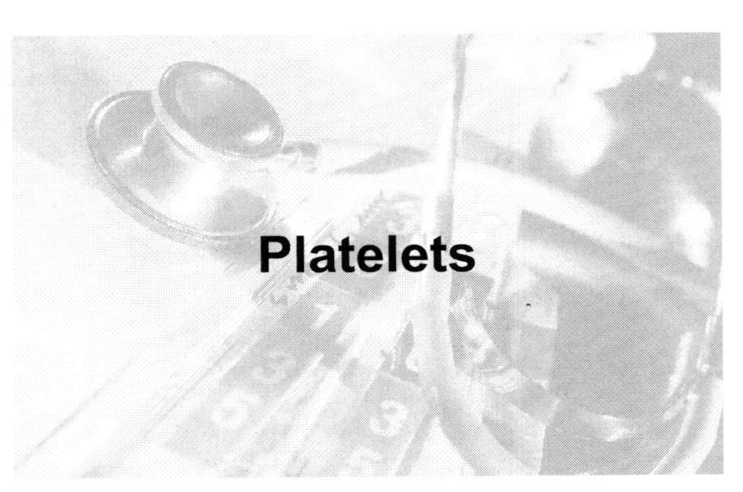
Platelets

Eustress

Incubation period

Anything which triggers a response from the immune system

Human chorionic gonadotrophin

A percentage of alcohol in a beverage

Newborn baby

Calming part of the nervous system

A positive form of stress

Responsible to clot and stop bleeding

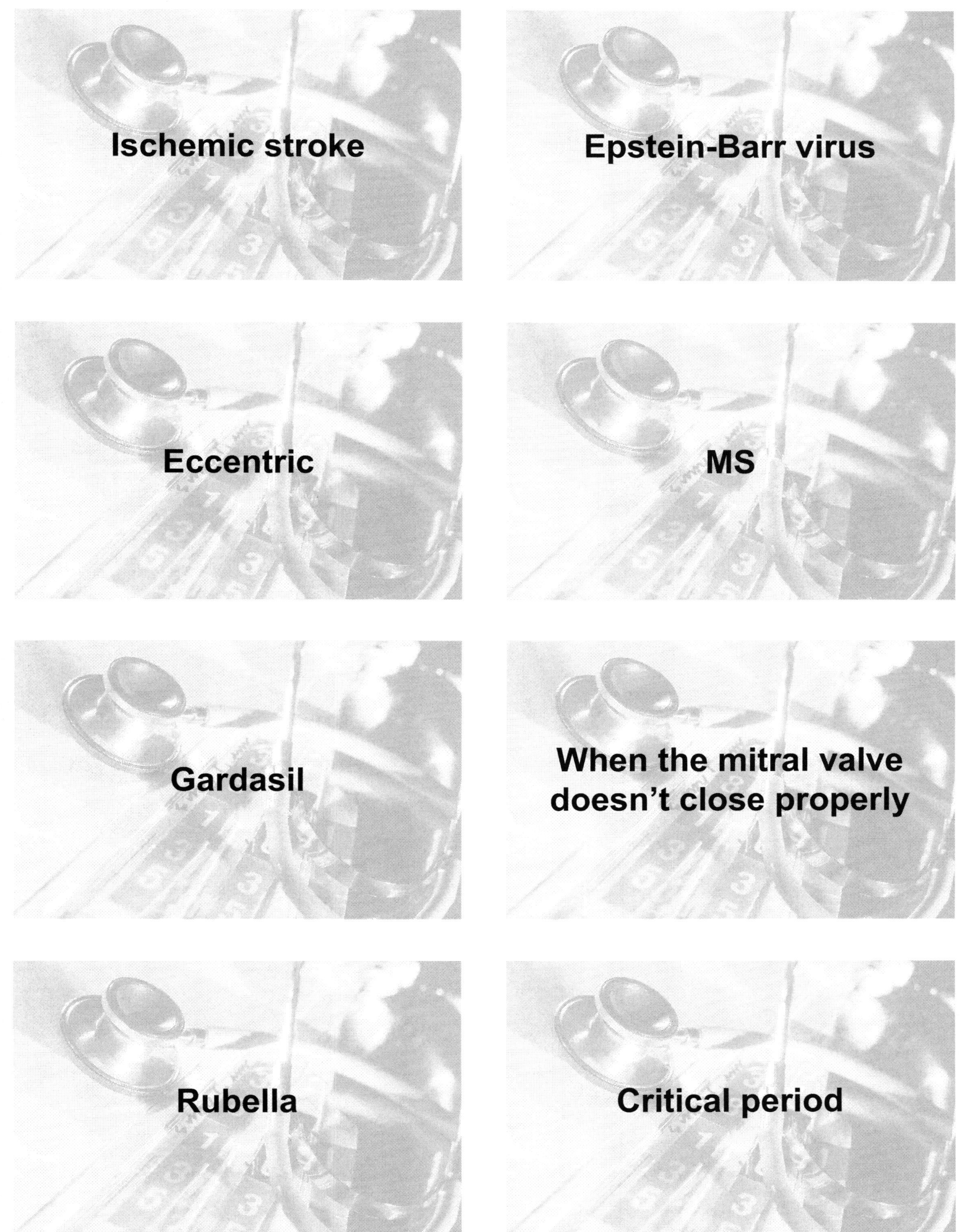
Ischemic stroke
Epstein-Barr virus
Eccentric
MS
Gardasil
When the mitral valve doesn't close properly
Rubella
Critical period

Can cause mononucleosis

Blockage to arteries leading to the brain

When a person's immune system begins to attack their nervous system

Force produced while the muscle is lengthening

Mitral Valve Prolapse

Approved vaccine for HPV in women

A time in development when a certain event will have the greatest impact

German measles

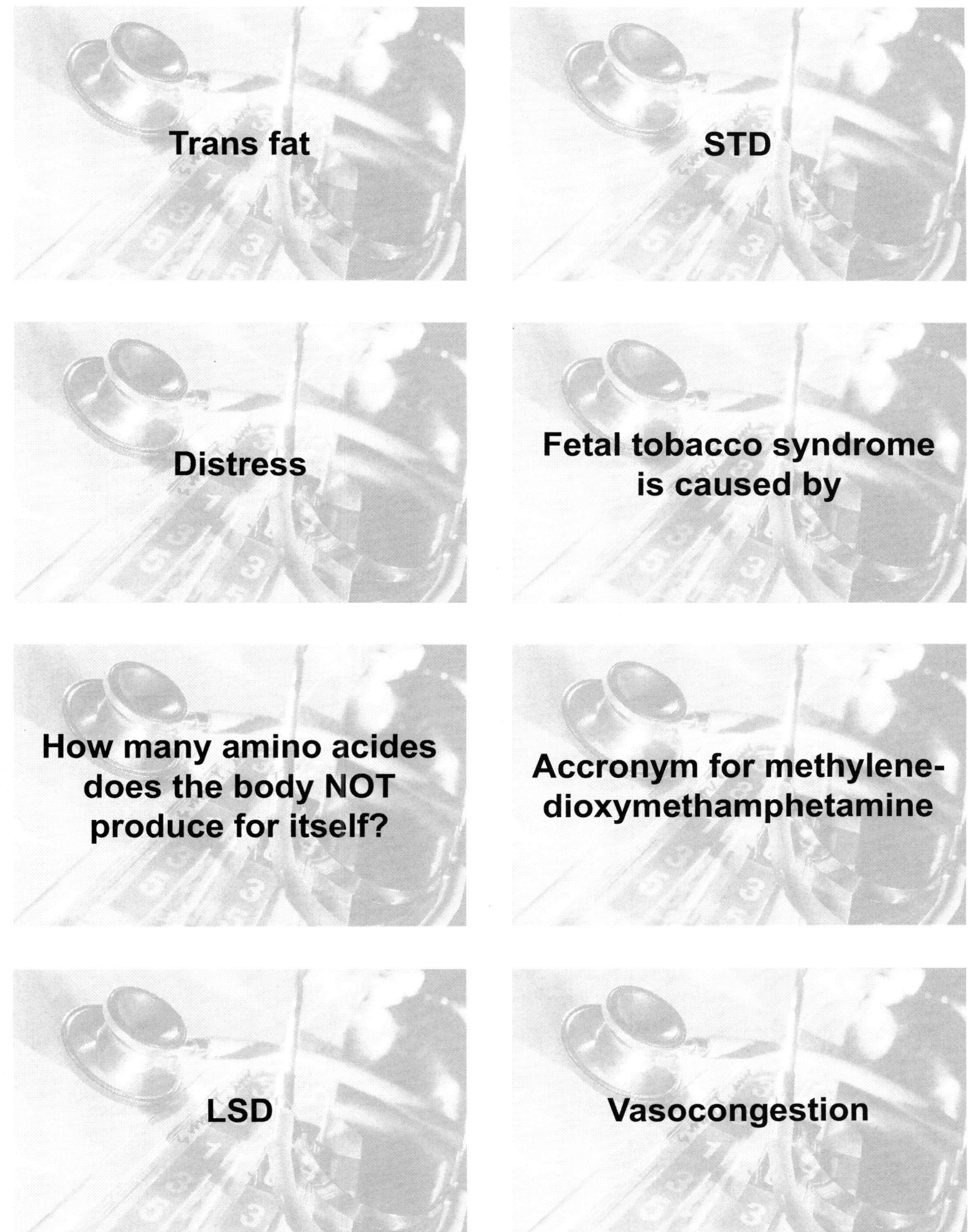
Trans fat
STD
Distress
Fetal tobacco syndrome is caused by
How many amino acides does the body NOT produce for itself?
Accronym for methylene-dioxymethamphetamine
LSD
Vasocongestion

Sexually transmitted diseases

Heightens a person's LDL (bad cholesterol) and lowers their HDL (good cholesterol)

Mother's smoking while pregnant

A bad form of stress

MDMA

9

Increased blood flow to an area of the body causing an increase in blood pressure and swelling of tissue

Acid

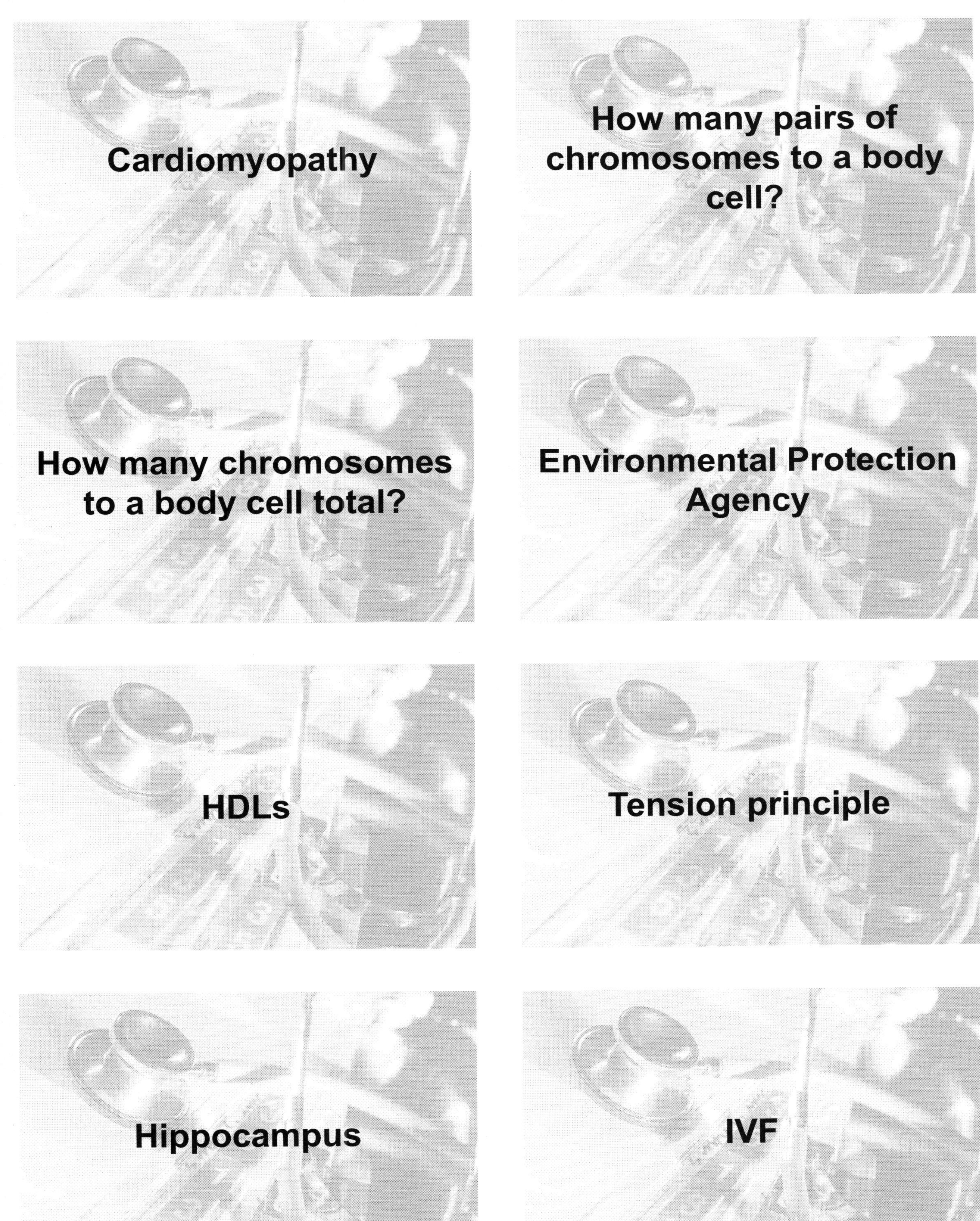
Cardiomyopathy
How many pairs of chromosomes to a body cell?
How many chromosomes to a body cell total?
Environmental Protection Agency
HDLs
Tension principle
Hippocampus
IVF

23 pairs

Any problem or disease which causes decreased function of the heart

EPA

46

The more tension you create in a muscle, the greater your strength will be

Good cholesterol

The most common assisted reproduction method

Memory section of the brain

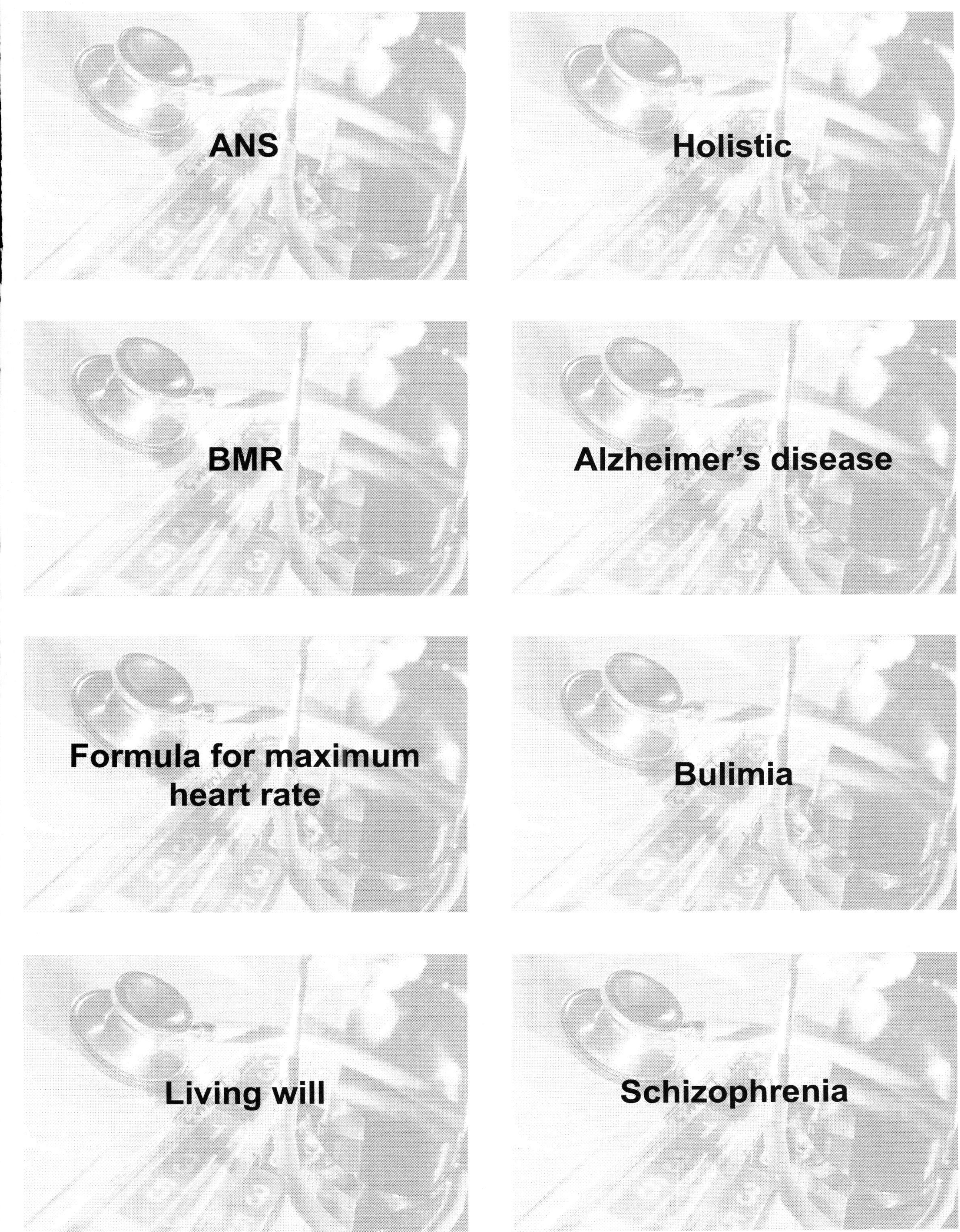
ANS
Holistic
BMR
Alzheimer's disease
Formula for maximum heart rate
Bulimia
Living will
Schizophrenia

Cure both the disease and the cause

Autonomic nervous system

When the brain begins to deteriorate in the areas controlling memory, speech, and personality

Basal metabolic rate

Binge and purge

220-age

Characterized by thinking in illogical and confused patterns, and withdrawing from reality

A document in which a person outlines what they want to be done as far as medical treatment in the event they become incapacitated

Made in the USA
Columbia, SC
25 March 2020

89958438R00087